GW00888606

Christmas Tinderbox

Starting points, stories, songs, activities

compiled by Sue Nicholls

DERBYSHIRE
COUNTY LIBRARY

Date **16 MAR 1989**

Class

SCHOOL LIBRARY SERVICE

A & C Black · London

Designed by Geoff Green
Cover and illustrations by Nita Sowter
Diagrams by Helen Herbert
Music setting by Words and Music Graphics,
   Southend-on-Sea
Printed by Hollen Street Press, Slough

First published 1986 by A & C Black (Publishers) Ltd
35 Bedford Row, London WC1R 4JH
© 1986 by A & C Black (Publishers) Ltd
Reprinted with corrections 1987

All rights reserved. No part of this publication may be
reproduced, stored in a retrieval system, or transmitted
in any form or by any means without the prior
permission of A & C Black (Publishers) Ltd.

Christmas Tinderbox: starting points, stories,
songs, activities.
1. Christmas   2. Christian education of children
I. Nicholls, Sue
372.19 BV1475.2

ISBN 0-7136-5557-7

Contents

Winter is icumen in

Snow poems 5, 10, 14
Winter poems 8, 10, 13, 14
Songs: Snow echo song 6
   Snow 12
   Five jolly snowmen 14
Making a forest picture or frieze 8
Stories and personal memories:
   Snow arrives in the Wild Wood 7
   The Snow Queen's Palace 9
   The most memorable snowfall of my life 10
   Winter in town and country 11
   Does Christmas mean winter? 11

Then there was a star danced
Light at the darkest time of year

To make: Pentagon star 15
   Egg-box lanterns 18
   Paper lanterns 26
Regent Street lights 16
Acrostics 16
Songs: Star in the velvet sky 18
   Star blaze 24
The lighthouse keeper's Christmas 19
Diwali 22
Hanukkah 23
Fire-flowers 25
Christmas tree lights 25

This Goodly Company
Christmas characters, real and mythical

Father Christmas stories:
   Father Christmas and the carpenter 27
   Father Christmas's clothes 34
If Santa Claus comes down the chimney
   (song) 30
Father Christmas: Up on the moon (poem) 32
Father Christmases to make: from card 32
   knitted 33
Kings, shepherds, angels:
   costumes 36
   to make 38, 39, 40
   Shepherds wake (song) 37
   The Kings 40
Good King Wenceslas 35
Sir Oswald 39
Baboushka 41
Scrooge and his nephew 41

Tis the season to be jolly
Customs and entertainments

As Christmas approaches:
   Advent calendar 42
   Christmas at School 43
   Christmas Eve (song) 44
Parties: Paul's Christmas birthday 46
   Let's make a party hat (song) 47
Carol-singing, apple-howling 48–49
Games: The game of Popp 50
   Charades and word-games 51

Christmas in hospital 50
Crackers 50
Decorations: Loop mobiles 52
Customs and origins: Christmas across Europe,
    Boxing Day, Saturnalia, Epiphany, Twelfth
    Night, the Lord of Misrule, Pantomimes,
    Mummers 52–53
Christmas echo song 54
New Year 56

We all want some figgy pudding
Christmas fare

To make: Surprise Christmas Pud 57
    St Nicholas letter biscuits 62
    Mincemeat slices 65
Songs and poems:
    The Robots' Christmas Dinner 57
    Christmas food song 58
    Mince pie calypso 64
Stories and memories 60, 61, 63
Customs and origins: Christmas pudding 62
    Meat, frumenty, mince pies 63
    Bean cake, Stir-up Sunday, Dumb cakes,
        Snapdragon 66

Robin's ruddy tum
Animals and birds

Robins and other birds:
    to make 67, 72
poems 68, 69
Robin Redbreast (song) 68
stories 69, 70
feeding in winter 71
Model animals for the stable scene 73
Reindeer: to make 74
    information 75
Animal stories:
    Why a donkey was chosen 73
    The big white pussy-cat 76
    Hugo at Sky Castle 78
    The legend of the spider's web 82
Anansi at Christmas 76
Mrs Malone 80
Farming at Christmas 82

All in a wood there grew a tree
Christmas trees and evergreens

To make: Cardboard roll tree 83
    Christmas tree biscuits 84
    Clay Christmas tree card 84
    Paper tree 85
    Silver snowflakes for the tree 87
    Cut-out Christmas tree card 89
    Mistletoe kissing bough 90
Poems 85, 91
Christmas tree, straight and tall (song) 86
Customs and origins 88, 90, 91

My true love gave to me
Gifts and giving

Stories: The new baby king 92
    Morris's disappearing bag 93
    A busy day 96
    Angels in hoods and mittens 97
    The elves and the shoemaker 102
    A gift for Gramps 104
    A new doll 105
    Papa Panov's special Christmas 106
Pass the parcel (song) 94
To make:
    Chocolate and coconut shortbread 95
    Knitted teddy 95
    Paper plate calendars 98
    Heart baskets 101
    Uncooked sweets 103
Christmas cards 98–101
Poems: Shops at Christmas 96
    Horace's Christmas disappointment 103
    Christmas thank yous 108
    Afterthought 108

Acknowledgements 109
Index of authors 110
Alphabetical list of contents 111
Subject index 112

Introduction

Christmas Tinderbox is primarily a teachers' resource book for use in infant and junior schools, an anthology of stories, poems, literary extracts, information, recipes and art and craft work. Some Christmas songs are included (most are published here for the first time) and also a number of personal accounts – insights into specific aspects of Christmas. All the material is arranged into eight topic-sections, each containing a cross-section of the different elements included in the book; this arrangement of material will be of particular interest to teachers and children who are accustomed to working within topics or projects that draw on all subject areas of the curriculum.

There are three indexes at the end: an author index, an alphabetical list of contents, and (the largest) a subject index.

I hope this book will provide teachers with a wealth of ideas to complement the programme of activities in their own schools and to enhance still further the enjoyment of the Christmas season.

Sue Nicholls

Winter is icumen in

Snowfall

Someone in the sky last night
Had an awful pillow fight,
And when I woke today I found
All the feathers on the ground.

Margaret Hillert

Snow Toward Evening

Suddenly the sky turned grey,
The day,
Which had been bitter and chill,
Grew soft and still.
Quietly
From some invisible blossoming tree
Millions of petals cool and white
Drifted and blew,
Lifted and flew,
Fell with the falling night.

Melville Cane

Winter Morning

Winter is the king of showmen,
Turning tree stumps into snow men
And houses into birthday cakes
And spreading sugar over lakes.
Smooth and clean and frosty white,
The world looks good enough to bite.
That's the season to be young,
Catching snowflakes on your tongue.

Snow is snowy when it's snowing,
I'm sorry it's slushy when it's going.

Ogden Nash

Snow

When winter winds blow
Hedges to and fro
And the flapping crow
Has gone to his home long ago,
Then I know
Snow
Will quietly fall, grow
Overnight higher than houses below,
Stop the stream in its flow,
And so
In a few hours, show
Itself man's ancient foe.
O
How slow
Is the silent gathering of snow.

Leonard Clark

Snow echo song

1 Snow, snow from on high,
Floating earthwards from the sky,
Falling on the town below
Gentle drifting freezing snow.

2 Soft and silent, not a sound
As it covers up the ground,
Even in the blackest night
Everything becomes so white.

   Snow, snow, soft and slow,
   Soft and slow,
   Snow,
   Snow.

Stuart Johnson

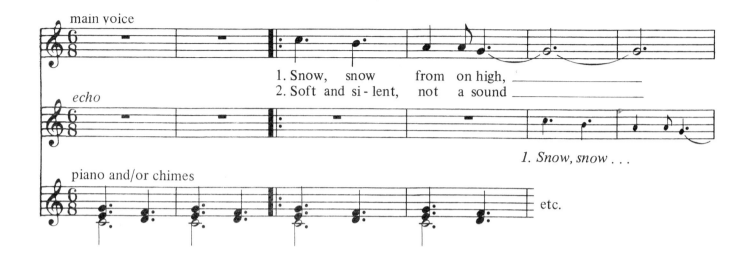

Soft and slow,____

Snow, snow . . .

Snow,   Snow.____   *voices die away*

Snow,   Snow.____   *voices die away*

keep repeating and fade out

The echo can be a second voice-part, or it can be played on recorders or high glocks.

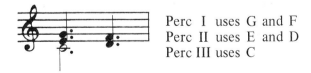

Perc I uses G and F
Perc II uses E and D
Perc III uses C

The accompaniment is a very simple ostinato – a figure which repeats unchanging throughout the song. It can be played on chime bars or other tuned percussion, using any number of players from two upwards.

Snow arrives in the Wild Wood

When at last the Mole woke up, much refreshed and in his usual spirits, the Rat said, 'Now then! I'll just take a look outside and see if everything's quiet, and then we really must be off.'

He went to the entrance of their retreat and put his head out. Then the Mole heard him saying quietly to himself, 'Hullo! hullo! here—*is*—a—go!'

'What's up, Ratty?' asked the Mole.

'*Snow* is up,' replied the Rat briefly; 'or rather *down*. It's snowing hard.'

The Mole came and crouched beside him, and, looking out, saw the wood that had been so dreadful to him in quite a changed aspect. Holes, hollows, pools, pitfalls, and other black menaces to the wayfarer were vanishing fast, and a gleaming carpet of faery was springing up everywhere, that looked too delicate to be trodden upon by rough feet. A fine powder filled the air and caressed the cheek with a tingle in its touch, and the black boles of the trees showed up in a light that seemed to come from below.

'Well, well, it can't be helped,' said the Rat, after pondering. 'We must make a start, and take our chance, I suppose. The worst of it is, I don't exactly know where we are. And now this snow makes everything look so very different.'

from The Wind in the Willows *by Kenneth Grahame*

Making a forest picture or frieze

This is a very effective picture that evokes a dark, leafless forest and may be easily achieved as follows:

A background comprising horizontal stripes of various colours (but not black) is painted on to sugar paper. While the stripes are still fresh, a damp brush is stroked lightly along the colour 'joins', resulting in a smudgy, tinted sky. This is a useful exercise for children who are still experimenting with mixing powder paints, for the consistency of the colours mixed is not crucial and the result is always pleasing.

When this is dry, a number of tree silhouettes (drawn freehand, not copied) are cut out of black, brown or grey paper, arranged on to the background with branches overlapping and then stuck on with glue.

These can be individual pictures or, if done on a large scale, they can be amalgamated into a classroom frieze.

In the Wood

Cold winter's in the wood,
  I saw him pass
Crinkling up fallen leaves
  Along the grass.

Bleak winter's in the wood,
  The birds have flown
Leaving the naked trees
  Shivering alone.

King Winter's in the wood,
  I saw him go
Crowned with a coronet
  Of crystal snow.

Eileen Mathias

A Winter's Day

Trees in the far-off distance,
White skeletons against a mauve grey sky.
Frost like icy sugar lumps on the spiky grass.
A cloudless blue sky above us,
Trees like filigree lace,
Making a cobweb against the turquoise.
White hedges like snow-capped mountains
By the golden pond.
Beneath the gay sun
Bulrushes like stiff needles
Pointing skywards.
Patches on the ploughed field
Glistening beneath the happy sky,
Like sugar resting on the ground.
Tall trees like steeples
White catkins hanging from the thin grey
  branches
Fluffy white flowers pointing downwards
Over the white graves.
A post card church, grey, mauve and gold
Against a clear sky.
Ghostly fingers of the walnut tree
No squirrels leaping gaily
Amongst the frost-covered branches.

children, 10 and 11

The Snow Queen's Palace

The story begins with a wicked magician who conjured up a magic mirror, wherein all beauty was reflected as base and ugly. This mirror was shattered and the fragments flew about the earth, causing havoc wherever they landed, for each speck retained the evil properties of the original looking-glass.

Two children, a boy named Kay, and girl, Gerda, were very close friends, but one winter's day two of the glass slivers entered Kay's eye and heart and he became cold and unfeeling towards Gerda and mocked her cruelly. That same evening the Snow Queen, a beautiful but wicked ice-lady, abducted Kay and swept him off to her palace.

Gerda follows Kay to rescue him and has many adventures on the way. Eventually her selfless determination prevails and she breaks the Snow Queen's spell. The two children then triumphantly return home.

The walls of the palace were formed of the drifted snow, its doors and windows of the cutting winds. There were more than a hundred rooms in the palace, the largest of them many miles in length. They were all lit up by the Northern Lights, and were all alike vast, empty, icily cold, and dazzlingly white. In the midst of the empty, endless hall of snow lay a frozen lake; it was broken into a thousand pieces, each piece so exactly like the others that the breaking of them might well be deemed a work of more than human skill. The Snow Queen, when at home, always sat in the middle of this lake.

Little Kay was quite blue, nay, almost black with cold, but he did not feel it, for the Snow Queen had kissed away the shiverings and his heart was already a lump of ice. He was busied among the sharp icy fragments, laying and joining them together in every possible way, just as people do with what are called Chinese puzzles. Kay could form the most curious and complete figures – and in his eyes they were of the utmost importance. He often formed whole words, but there was one word he could never succeed in forming – it was Eternity. The Snow Queen said to him 'When you can put that together, you shall be your own master and I will give you the whole world, and a new pair of skates besides.' But he could never do it.

'Now I am going to the warmer countries,' said the Snow Queen. 'I shall flit through the air, and look into the black craters, as they are called, of Etna and Vesuvius. I shall whiten them a little. That will be good for the lemons and the vines.' So away flew the Snow Queen, leaving Kay sitting all alone in the large, empty hall of ice.

He looked at the pieces of ice and thought and thought till his head ached. He sat so still and so stiff that one might have thought that he too was frozen.

Cold and cutting blew the winds when little Gerda passed through the palace gates, but she repeated her evening prayer, and they at once sank to rest. She entered the large empty hall and saw Kay. She knew him at once. She flew to him and fell upon his neck, and held him fast, and cried, 'Kay! Dear, dear Kay! I have found you at last!'

But he sat still, quite stiff and cold and motionless. His unkindness wounded poor Gerda. She wept bitterly and her hot tears fell on his breast and thawed the ice, and penetrated to his heart and washed out the splinter of glass. He looked at her whilst she sang:

'Though roses bloom, then fade away and die,
The Christ-Child's face we yet shall see on high.'

Then Kay burst into tears. He wept till the glass splinter floated in his eye and fell with his tears. Then he knew his old companion, and cried with joy, 'Gerda, my dear little Gerda, where have you been all this time? – and where have I been?'

from The Snow Queen *by Hans Andersen*

Night in Bethlehem

The moon shines on pebbled streets
late travellers knock on doors
the town is dark and still.

The bright yellow windows turn black
as the lights go out one by one
and all is still in the sleepy town.

No more sounds of children playing
but a baby cries in a house
and a dog barks in the darkness.

Straw rustles in the stables
as the animals settle down
sleepy and tired in the dark.

The foal snuggles up to his mother
and the donkey brays loudly
smelling his warm oats.

The stars appear one by one
and glitter in the sky
frost shines on the ground.

Now all is quiet
night is here
the stars glitter

the moon shines.
And on the cold hillside
the lonely shepherds guard their sheep.

Children, 7 and 8

The most memorable snowfall of my life

The war was over. 1945 had been an exciting year. There had been street parties, victory parades, soldiers coming home and the occasional orange and banana about if your Mum queued for them. And then the following year came the snow. Such a snowfall, not a few inches, but sufficient to be measured in feet! An absolute wonderland for a seven year old. I would go out and play in it for about ten minutes and then come in to warm my hands, which I can remember throbbed with cold from the snow. We all vied to make the largest snowball. One of the boys won. His must have stood five feet high.

On the first Sunday of the great snowfall it happened...There were about twelve of us playing when two of the Dads came out and began to bombard us with snowballs. Gradually other Dads came out and joined in. This Children versus Fathers snowball fight seemed to go on for hours, though in retrospect it probably lasted for just a short time.

The snow lingered on until it was piled up in the gutters, dirty and brown and too icy to play with. I am sure that there were unfortunate people with burst water pipes and cold houses but for one little girl it was the most memorable snowfall of them all.

Phyllis Lewis

Snow stars

The air is full of flying stars,
The sky is shaking down
A million silver stars of snow
On wood and field and town.

Frances Frost

Winter – in town...

The cold became intense. In the main street at the corner of the court, some labourers were repairing the gas-pipes, and had lighted a great fire in a brazier, round which a party of ragged men and boys were gathered: warming their hands and winking their eyes before the blaze in rapture. The water-plug being left in solitude, its overflowings sullenly congealed, and turned to misanthropic ice. The brightness of the shops where holly sprigs and berries crackled in the lamp heat of the windows, made pale faces ruddy as they passed. Poulterers' and grocers' trades became a splendid joke: a glorious pageant with which it was next to impossible to believe that such dull principles as bargain and sale had anything to do. The Lord Mayor, in the stronghold of the mighty Mansion House, gave orders to his fifty cooks and butlers to keep Christmas as a Lord Mayor's household should; and even the little tailor, whom he had fined five shillings on the previous Monday for being drunk and bloodthirsty in the streets, stirred up tomorrow's pudding in his garret, while his lean wife and the baby sallied out to buy the beef.

from A Christmas Carol *by Charles Dickens*

...and country

Now the winter's day was set in motion and we rode through its crystal kingdom. We examined the village for its freaks of frost, for anything we might use. We saw the frozen spring by the side of the road, huge like a swollen flower. Water-wagtails hovered above it, nonplussed at its silent hardness, and again and again they dropped down to drink, only to go sprawling in a tumble of feathers. We saw the stream in the valley, black and halted, a tarred path threading through the willows. We saw trees lopped-off by their burdens of ice, cow-tracks like pot-holes in rock, quiet lumps of sheep licking the spiky grass with their black and rotting tongues. The church clock had stopped and the weather-cock was frozen, so that both time and the winds were stilled; and nothing, we thought, could be more exciting than this; interference by a hand unknown, the winter's No to routine and laws – sinister, awesome, welcome.

from Cider with Rosie *by Laurie Lee*

Does Christmas mean winter?

Is your Christmas a time of cold, wintery weather and dark evenings, a time to stay indoors? Not for everyone: Mark Rosen writes from Papua New Guinea:

Christmas Day some of us drove into the hills and spent a pleasant morning walking through the forest. We then had a bar-b-q lunch on the edge of a great escarpment looking down to the sparkling sea. It was refreshingly cool up in the hills.

We've had some excellent walking weather, and on New Year's Day we had a magical walk along the hilltops parallel to the coast. On our west was the sea – vivid blue and turquoise and aquamarine, and so clear we could peer down to the coral on the bottom. And we watched two schools of tuna chasing shoals of little fish. To our east was a broad and green valley, and then a dramatic skyline of mountains – so clear we could pick out places we had flown to and walked at week-ends. It was such a beautiful walk – you would have loved it. And the finale was a very steep descent to the beach, a stroll along the shell-strewn strand, to a sandy bay where we swam and swam till rather burnt by the sun – and then piled into my bus, which I'd parked there very early that day, and drove back to Moresby.

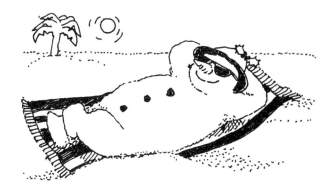

Snow

1 Snow, snow, falling down,
   Making hardly any sound.
   Crystal patterns on the glass,
   Snowy carpet on the grass.
       Snow, snow, snow.
       Snow, snow, snow.

2 Snow, snow, swirling round,
   Silent snowflakes touch the ground.
   Frosty shapes on window panes,
   Icy fingers in the drains.
       Snow, snow, snow.
       Snow, snow, snow.

3 Snow, snow, bright and white,
   Making such a lovely sight,
   Crisp and clean and cold and still,
   Children love it, always will.
       Snow, snow, snow.
       Snow, snow, snow.

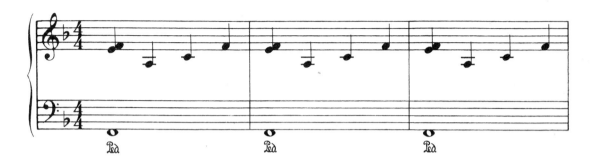

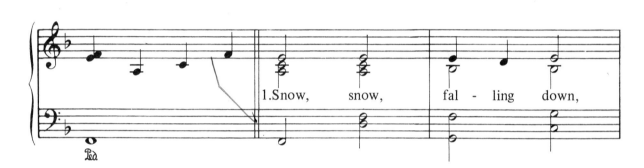

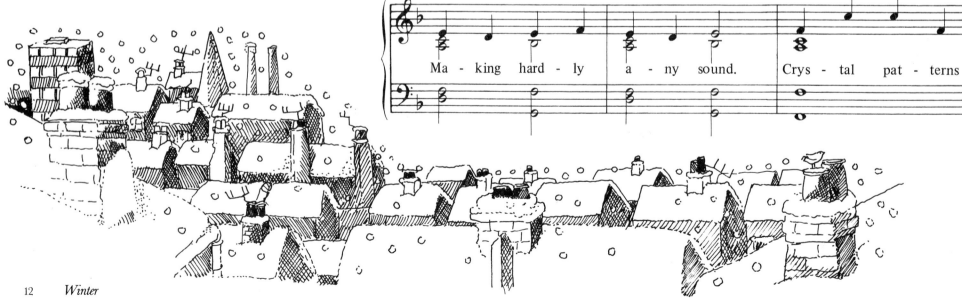

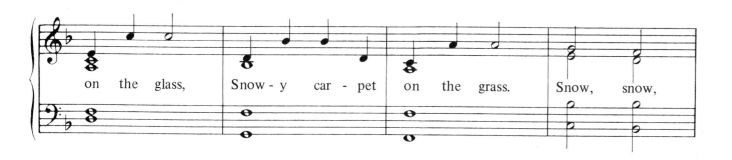

on the glass, Snow-y car - pet on the grass. Snow, snow,

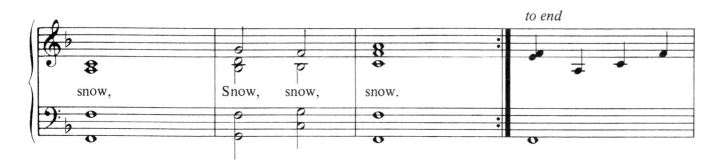

to end

snow, Snow, snow, snow.

Stan Gordon

Winter Days

Biting air
Winds blow
City streets
Under snow

Noses red
Lips sore
Runny eyes
Hands raw

Chimneys smoke
Cars crawl
Piled snow
On garden wall

Slush in gutters
Ice in lanes
Frosty patterns
On window panes

Morning call
Lift up head
Nipped by winter
Stay in bed

Gareth Owen

First Snow

Snow makes whiteness where it falls.
The bushes look like popcorn-balls.
And places where I always play
Look like somewhere else today.

Marie Louise Allen

Winter Morning

No one has ever been here before,
Never before!
Snow is stretching, pure and white,
From the back door
To where that elm-tree by the coppice-fence
Stands black and bare,
With never a footprint, never a clawprint
Anywhere!
Only the clean, white page of snow
In front of me,
With the long shadow of a single tree
For company.

Clive Sansom

There was an old person of Mold

There was an old person of Mold
Who shrank from sensations of cold;
So he purchased some muffs,
Some furs and some fluffs,
And wrapped himself from the cold.

Edward Lear

Five jolly snowmen

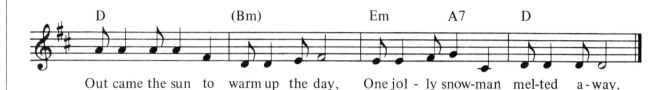

Five jolly snowmen ready to play,
Ready to play, ready to play.
Out came the sun to warm up the day,
One jolly snowman melted away.

Four jolly snowmen ready to play . . .

SN

Five children line up representing the five snowmen.
On the words 'melted away' one child sits down.

Suggested percussion accompaniment:

claves: ♪ ♩ ♪ ♩ ♩ throughout

tambourine: shaken during the last two bars of
each verse

Then there was a star danced

Light at the darkest time of year

Pentagon star

This version of a Christmas star gives children the opportunity of drawing the outline themselves rather than relying on the overworked template.

Begin by drawing round a pentagon (readily found in boxes of attribute blocks) on a large sheet of thin card. Rest a ruler along one of the pentagon's sides and extend the line at each end. Do the same for each of the remaining four sides. The extensions will cross each other and form the points of a star.

Use large and small pentagons to give you different sized stars. Spray or paint them silver and gold (on both sides) and suspend them from a hoop covered with crepe paper on varying lengths of string. This makes an eye-catching mobile.

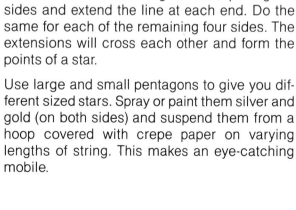

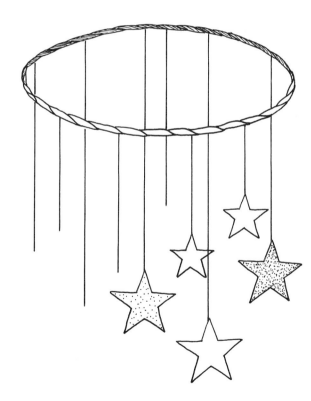

Regent Street Lights

Regent Street has always attracted thousands of visitors, particularly at Christmas time. In 1954 the now world-acclaimed Christmas decorations were started, and for many years they were the brain child of a designer called Beverly Pick.

In 1971, after eighteen years, the Lights went out for what everyone thought would be the last time, due to lack of funds. But in 1977, the Queen's Silver Jubilee Year, the Council of the Regent Street Association began to discuss the idea of bringing the Lights back into the West End. Christmas trade that year was slow and it was felt that the return of the Lights might stimulate the return of the visitors. Gradually, over the next few months, it was decided that in 1978 the 'Spirit of Christmas' would be brought back to the West End.

The process of planning the Lights is a fairly long one and it starts in January with a number of designers submitting designs. Some are asked for by the Association and some hear via the grapevine and approach the Association independently. The Council see the designs several times before choosing the final one.

Once it has been chosen costings have to be done, manufacturing problems worked out, safety factors adhered to, permissions granted by various local authorities and, most important of all, the money for the project has to be collected from all the shops and businesses in the street.

1978 was a particularly exciting year, the year the Lights returned. The installers, Piggotts, were faced with the daunting task of re-doing the anchor points on the roof tops and the facings of the buildings to accommodate new safety regulations laid down by the District Surveyors. In May the Association decided that they would like the Prince of Wales to switch on the Lights – if possible on November 14th, his birthday. They were fortunate enough to be honoured with a 'yes'. The Street was aglow that night: the press out in force as it was His Royal Highness's 30th birthday; the whole ceremony televised live; bands and choirs, and crowds in the street. The West End was alive and it was an occasion that many people will long remember.

Acrostics

These provide a simple framework for creative writing. They are particularly useful for younger writers who are less able to write at length, or for any lesson when time is short. For older children acrostics present the challenge of composing sentences economically. This medium can be extended for more fluent and imaginative writers by adding a rhyming element or perhaps by limiting the number of words or syllables per line.

Giving presents round the tree,
Is that large round one for me?
Father Christmas brought them here
To bring our family Christmas cheer!

Acrostics can also be incorporated into art work:

Snowball head,
Nose is a carrot,
Old hat to wear,
Woolly scarf next,
Make eyes from coal,
After the thaw
Nothing remains.

Lights keep the streets bright
I put the lights on when it's dark
Good candles can make it very bright
Happy lights go on christmas trees
STreet lights help you see the way

Jacqueline James, 7

Candles are made out of wax.
A candle gives a small light.
New candles can be different colours.
Dim candles give a very faint light.
Lighted candles can be very dangerous if they are knocked over.
Every candle has a black wick.

Joanna Yu, 8

Star in the velvet sky

Partner song to *Twinkle twinkle little star* with descant recorder accompaniment

Star in the velvet sky,
Winking your silver eye,
Showing from up on high
Where the saviour lies.

Like some precious gem,
Shining on Bethlehem,
Let your signal bright
Lead the kings through the night.

Star in the velvet sky,
Winking your silver eye,
Showing from up on high
Where the saviour lies.

SN

The 'star' song—the top line—should be taught first, and must be secure before other parts are added. The following introduction, which can be played on tuned percussion or recorders, provides the starting notes for both the sung parts, and will also set the tempo:

The hummed part (Twinkle, twinkle little star) should be very soft and sustained. If the piece is incorporated into a Christmas concert the audience might be invited to hum this part.

let your sig-nal bright lead the kings through the night.

Star in the vel-vet sky, wink-ing your sil-ver eye,

show-ing from up on high where the sa-viour lies.

Egg box lanterns

These 3-D lanterns, which use the clear plastic variety of egg boxes, are very striking and can be tackled by the youngest children.

You will need two clear plastic egg boxes for each lantern and some tissue scraps and other materials for decoration.

Open the egg boxes and join (e.g staple) them together along the edges to give a four-sided box lantern. Decorate by crumpling coloured tissue paper to stick into the egg-box pockets and add a fringe of tissue, crêpe paper or foil to the bottom edges. The finished lanterns can then be hung by thread.

The Lighthouse Keeper's Christmas

It is the middle of December and a gale is blowing. The sky is dark although it is mid-day and the sea is the colour of lead with long white streaks of windblown spume scarring the surface.

The sort of day to put some more coal on the fire and curl up in front of it with a book if you do not HAVE to go out.

But there are people who DO have to go out and the Keeper returning to the Lighthouse is one of them.

His period of leave is over and he huddles in the shelter of the buildings at the tiny airfield waiting for the sound of the approaching helicopter above the howling wind. Eventually the helicopter comes into view, its navigation lights flashing and twinkling in the gloom. Lower and lower it descends, facing the buffeting wind until it lands, not too far from the waiting Keeper and his trolley loaded with boxes of stores.

This year he will be spending Christmas at the Lighthouse with two colleagues already out there, and the boxes contain all the food they will need for the next month . . . together with some 'extras' for Christmas Day. Once all the boxes are stowed into the cargo space of the helicopter the Keeper climbs in through a side door and sits on a bench seat behind the pilot and engineer. The rotor blades spin faster and faster and the tiny helicopter is in the air once more and is immediately blown sideways with the force of the gale – but the pilot skilfully corrects the course and heads for the "Tower" some six miles out in the Atlantic Ocean.

After a few minutes flying they see it, looking very like a tall factory chimney standing all alone in the sea but with a lot of scaffolding around the top. As they get nearer the 'scaffolding' is revealed as a strong steel structure supporting a platform on which the helicopter will land. The platform doesn't look very big but as they approach they see that it is quite large enough for their helicopter.

After landing all the boxes are unloaded and lowered through hatches in the landing platform to the Keepers waiting below. When all this has been done the Keeper going home climbs into the helicopter, taking the place of the Keeper reporting for duty. A quick wave from the pilot and the helicopter zooms up and away, heading for land again.

On the Lighthouse the Keepers begin the task of emptying the boxes and stowing away the meat in the freezer or the 'fridge. As they do so they are chatting eagerly and passing on the latest bits of news from ashore and from the other Lighthouses. Then, as they open one box, they find a letter inside. It's from the local Round Table/Rotary Clubs informing them that this is a hamper donated specially to the Keepers who will be away from home this Christmas. Apart from a plump fowl they find a big cake and a super box of crackers. Everything else in the hamper is in threes . . . three tins of fruit, three small Christmas puddings, three net 'stockings' of oranges, apples and nuts, and so on ensuring that each man gets an equal share of the 'goodies'. This may not be the only 'present' the Keepers get because sometimes the local Church will send out a hamper and occasionally lighthouses get "adopted" by Guides or Brownie Packs or schools who will send letters and cards to let the Keepers know that they will not be forgotten. It looks as though the Keepers will have a splendid time after all because, of course, they have all got presents from their own families too.

But, in the meantime, the work of the Lighthouse must go on. Every morning when the sun is above the horizon the light is extinguished and heavy curtains hung down the interior of the lantern to protect the 'Optic' from the sun. The Optic is a series of very strong lenses some six feet in diameter mounted in a bronze and steel rotating framework weighing about two and a half tonnes. It is massive and as soon as the curtains have been hung the Keeper sets out to dust and polish it and oil the machinery and generally see that all is ready for lighting up later that evening.

Different days bring different tasks designed to keep the Lighthouse in tip top condition. One day is given over to washing the glazing – the 'windows' of the lantern – and although the insides are easy it is a different matter when the Keeper has to clean the outsides, one hundred and eighty feet above the sea!!! Then there are the engines and electric generators to clean and overhaul so that they are ready for use at a moments notice. Every day the floors will be swept and washed all the way down from the lantern to the entrance door – eight flights of curving stairs down! Only when the Keeper has finished all his routine duties is he free to spend time on his hobby or even just reading. Nowadays every lighthouse has radio and colour television but Keepers still will often spend time together playing games like chess, cards or dominoes.

Christmas time is the time when they really 'get-together'.

A couple of days before Christmas they put up a few streamers and decorations in the sitting room and display all the cards they have received. From the cupboard under the stairs they retrieve the old plastic Christmas tree that they have had for years. A few baubles and bits of tinsel and the room takes on quite a festive air. All at once it is Christmas.

At breakfast the Keepers greet each other, exchange little gifts and, as soon as breakfast is over, start to unwrap the presents from their families. There are "Oooh's" and "Aaah's" and "Blow-me-downs" intermingled with the laughter as the brightly coloured wrapping paper covers the floor. Over the extra cup of coffee they sit silent and their eyes glaze a little as they perhaps picture their own children opening presents under the Christmas tree at home.

"Come on, shift yerselves," calls one Keeper, "Can't sit 'ere all day." He is 'Cook-of-the-Day' today and there is a bird to get in the oven, a pudding to steam, potatoes to roast and sprouts to boil and a hundred and one things that go towards dinner on Christmas Day. The other two leave the Kitchen and take the opportunity to telephone home their "Merry Christmas"'s to their respective families.

Christmas dinner is superb. The bird is done to a turn, the stuffing mouth-watering. The 'taters are brown and crisp and the pudding with brandy sauce . . . Mmmm! They really enjoy it and pretend not to notice the pile of pans and dishes in the sink waiting to be washed up.

Eventually when every cup is back on its hook and every pan in its place in the rack the Keepers retire to the sitting room where they will relax for a while. Coloured paper hats are donned as they pull a cracker or two. Then out come the 'once-a-year' fat cigars that seem to signify Christmas to a lot of men – and possibly a glass of home-made wine as they sit back and listen to the Queen on the 'telly'.

After the Queen's Speech they jump up and turn on the radio transmitter. It has been a tradition ever since radio was introduced that, on Christmas afternoon, each lighthouse will, on a special frequency, call up the neighbouring lights – some may be up to a hundred miles away – and in turn will serenade each other with a carol or two that they have rehearsed. How the families ashore enjoy it for they too have been listening in on the radio back home and for a few minutes the Keepers do not seem too far away after all.

But soon the reality of their position is brought home to the Keepers again as the approaching dusk tells them it is time to 'light-up'. The Keeper on duty will go down to the engine room near the base of the Tower and start up one of the powerful diesel engines that powers a large electric generator. When everything is running smoothly he toils up the stairs again all the way up to the Lantern. There he takes down the heavy protective curtains, switches on the electric motor to rotate the Optic and then, after testing the 'Standby lamp', throws the switch to light the 'main' lamp of some 3,500 watts. The blinding light is magnified by the lenses in the Optic, and rhythmic, monotonous spokes of light are revolving out over the sea. All night the five million candlepower beams will signal to passing ships the location of the lighthouse and signpost a safe passage for them.

In the kitchen the kettle has boiled again and a pot of strong tea is brewed. The remainder of the bird is eaten, and the cake is cut and shared out with a bowl of fruit and cream for each man.

After tea it is back to the sitting room again for more crackers and nuts and television for the rest of the evening – except for one man. He is on duty and often must leave the room to check the light . . . the engines . . . the visibility – for even the slightest gathering of mist will alert him to prepare the Fog Signal machinery.

Hopefully that will not be necessary but he notices that the barometer is reading lower and they may be in for another gale. "Ah well," he thinks, "We aren't going anywhere for a while anyway, and here inside the Lighthouse we are warm and safe. I'm Cook-of-the-Day tomorrow, Boxing Day, and there's that leg of pork and parsnips and apple sauce . . . Merry Christmas!"

Andy Bluer

Principal Keeper, Pendeen Lighthouse, Cornwall

Winter festivals

When winter closes in and days are short, *light* becomes all the more significant and precious, and not surprisingly the religious festivals of Christmas, Diwali and Hanukkah all touch on this theme in their symbols and customs.

Diwali

The festival called Diwali is celebrated during the Hindu month of Karttika which usually coincides with November. It takes its name from a Sanskrit word 'Deepavali' meaning a row of lights. Diwali marks the return of Rama coming to reclaim his kingdom and the lights that people put in their windows are a sign of welcome to the king.

Rama, drawn from a 14th century South Indian bronze

Diwali in Bombay

The preparations for Diwali start well in advance. Three weeks before Diwali is Dussehra – the day when giant effigies of ten-headed Ravana are burnt on bonfires throughout India. Fireworks begin on that day and can be heard intermittently but with more intensity as Diwali approaches.

At home housewives are very busy since the whole house must be thoroughly cleaned before the New Year begins. Floors are washed, furniture polished, lamps cleaned and a few days before Diwali the cooking begins. Each family has its own favourite food but without doubt Diwali means eating and giving sweets.

Besides receiving sweets from neighbours and friends each worker receives a bonus from his/her workplace. This usually means one month's salary. Servants receive the same bonus; for example, the cleaner, the dhobi (washerman), the milkman, the paper boy, the sweeper, the driver and the cook – all get their bonuses. All work extremely well during the weeks preceding Diwali and receive their money with great rejoicing.

Most people go shopping for new clothes, toys and especially fireworks – the noisier the better.

During Diwali almost every house is alight with twinkling diyas (small homemade lamps) and in large houses electric lights of all colours brighten the darkness from dusk until dawn. The noise is incredible. Youngsters seem to vie with one another for the loudest 'banger'.

The day after Diwali is New Year's Day when people pray to Lakshmi, the Goddess of Wealth. Those who run businesses open their new accounts on that day with prayers to Lakshmi.

The two days are public holidays in India but every shop is open and people go out, spend money and enjoy themselves. It is a happy occasion when the evenings are becoming cooler and families and friends celebrate the return of Rama and Sita – the triumph of light over darkness.

Judith Bijlani

Song suggestion

Diwali (*Tinderbox* 62)

Hanukkah

In our home, the month of December is looked forward to with a great deal of excitement – particularly by our two children Carl and Lisa. For December brings an eight-day Jewish Festival called Hanukkah – the Festival of Lights.

It reminds us of a wonderful story which began thousands of years ago when the Jewish people were ruled over by the Syrians. The Syrians at the time had adopted Greek ways, and wanted everyone to behave as they did and to worship the Greek gods and statues. The Jews believed in just one God and refused to obey. To punish them the Syrians attacked the Holy City of Jerusalem, destroyed the Temple and killed many Jews. An old man named Mattathias fled to the mountains with his five sons and called on other Jews to join them. They formed a small army under the leadership of one of the sons, Judas Maccabee, and after several years they defeated the larger and much more powerful Syrian army and re-entered the Holy City. The Temple was rebuilt but when it came to finding enough oil to rekindle the everlasting light which hung over the altar, only enough linseed oil could be found to last for one day. A messenger was sent out for more oil and although it took him eight days to return, the oil miraculously kept burning. And so to remind us of this we celebrate Hanukkah by lighting candles for eight days.

We use a special candlestick called a Menorah which has eight branches for the Hanukkah lights plus another holder for the 'server' candle which is lit first and then used to light the others. Each evening our whole family gathers around the Menorah to say the special Hanukkah prayer and on each night we light an extra candle so that by the eighth night all the Hanukkah candles are burning brightly. We sing Hanukkah songs too, some in Hebrew and some in English, and play a special Hanukkah game with a four-sided spinning top called a 'dreidl' (pronounced draydel). We use hazelnuts as prizes; which side of the dreidl lands face-up determines whether you win all, half, or none of the nuts (or whether you have to hand over some of your winnings). Somehow Carl and Lisa always seem to end up with a mouthful of nuts!

In our family we also give presents at Hanukkah – small gifts each night – perhaps a book, a jigsaw or a game, ending on the eighth night with a 'big' present which is always one for our two children to share. We leave them on their beds and after we have lit the candles and had our 'sing-song' there is a mad dash upstairs to see what the present is for that Hanukkah night.

So as you can hear, the Festival of Lights – Hanukkah – is a very happy and noisy time for us, and that wonderful story of bravery and belief in God that we are remembering in our home in England is being remembered and celebrated with the lighting of candles by Jewish families all over the world.

Barbara Weintroub

Song suggestion

Hanukah (*Harlequin* 39)

Star light, star bright,
First star I see tonight.
Wish I may, wish I might
Have the wish I wish tonight.

Star blaze

1 Star shining bright,
   Star shining bright,
   Twinkling in the night,
   Twinkling in the night,
   Casting a ray and making it like day.
   Casting a ray and making it like day.
   Wonderful star
   Wonderful star
   Glowing from afar,
   Glowing from afar,
   No one has seen the heaven so serene.
   No one has seen the heaven so serene.

2 Star up on high,
   Star up on high,
   Diamond of the sky,
   Diamond of the sky,
   Jewel of the night, you give a wondrous light.
   Jewel of the night, you give a wondrous light.
   Blazing a trail,
   Blazing a trail,
   Showing without fail
   Showing without fail
   Where we must go through all the winter snow.
   Where we must go through all the winter snow.

star Glow-ing from a - far, *Glow-ing from a - far,*

No - one has seen the hea - ven so se - rene.

No - one has seen the hea - ven so se - rene.

Douglas Coombes

Fire-flowers

There is a Mexican legend that tells of a young girl waiting outside the church on Christmas Eve. She had no gift to take to the crib for she was too poor. There was a stone figure of an angel by the door, almost covered with weeds. The child began to pull them up when she heard a voice telling her to take the weeds to the crib where they, and she, would be blessed. She did so and as she entered the church the weeds became a brilliant red, as if they were on fire. Although these flowers are now called Poinsettias, many people still refer to them as Fire-flowers.

Christmas tree lights

The tiny candles originally used to light Christmas trees looked attractive but caused many dangerous fires. No alternative was discovered until an American telephone operator realised that the tiny bulbs on his switchboard would make an excellent substitute for candles. His ingenuity meant that live flames could be abandoned, and since then electric lights with miniature coloured bulbs have been manufactured specifically for Christmas trees.

More songs to sing

Christmas candles (*Count me in* 18)

Under Bethlehem's star so bright (*Carol gaily carol* 38)

Now light one thousand Christmas lights (*Carol gaily carol* 39)

Star in the south (*Merrily to Bethlehem* 22)

Lanterns

You will need:
  stiff black paper
  coloured tissue paper
  glue
  scissors
  cotton wool

Make a lantern template as shown, approximately 20cm tall and 15cm wide, taking care to make it symmetrical.

Cut out two lantern shapes in black paper.

Cut tissue squares to be windows, cutting them with 1cm spare all round for gluing.

Stick the tissue windows onto one of the lantern shapes.

Stick the other lantern shape over the first, so that the tissue windows are trapped between the two layers.

Roll small lengths of cotton wool and stick these on the bottom ledge of each window.

The lanterns can be hung, or stuck onto window panes.

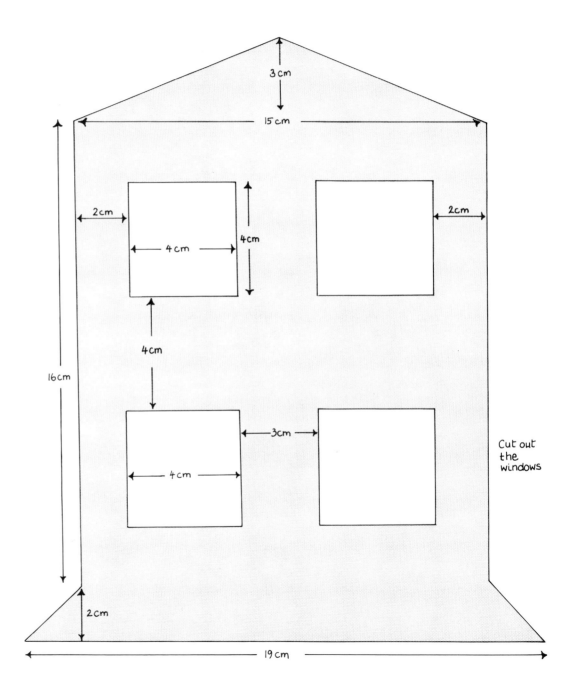

This Goodly Company

Christmas characters, real and mythical

Father Christmas and the Carpenter

There was once a carpenter called Anderson. He was a good father and he had a lot of children.

One Christmas Eve, while his wife and children were decorating the Christmas tree, Anderson crept out to his wood-shed. He had a surprise for them all; he was going to dress up as Father Christmas, load a sack of presents on to his sledge and go and knock on the front door. But as he pulled the loaded sledge out of the wood-shed, he slipped and fell across the sack of presents. This set the sledge moving, because the ground sloped from the shed down to the road, and Anderson had no time to shout "Way there!" before he crashed into another sledge which was coming down the road.

"I'm very sorry," said Anderson.

"Don't mention it; I couldn't stop myself," said the other man. Like Anderson, he was dressed in Father Christmas clothes and had a sack on his sledge.

"We seem to have the same idea," said Anderson. "I see you're all dressed up like me." He laughed and shook the other man by the hand. "My name is Anderson."

"Glad to meet you," said the other. "I'm Father Christmas."

"Ha, ha!" laughed Anderson. "You will have your little joke, and quite right too on Christmas Eve."

"That's what I thought," said the other man, "and if you will agree we can change places tonight, and that will be a better joke still; I'll take the presents along to your children if you'll go and visit mine. But you must take off that costume."

Anderson looked a bit puzzled. "What am I to dress up in, then?"

"You don't need to dress up at all," said the other. "My children see Father Christmas all the year round, but they've never seen a real carpenter. I told them last Christmas that if they were good this year I'd try to get a carpenter to come and see them while I went round with presents for human children."

"So he really is Father Christmas," thought Anderson to himself. Out loud he said, "All right, if you really want me to, I will. The only thing is, I haven't any presents for your children."

"Presents?" said Father Christmas. "Aren't you a carpenter?"

"Yes, of course."

"Well, then, all you have to do is to take along a few pieces of wood, and some nails. You have a knife, I suppose?" Anderson said he had and went to look for the things in his workshop.

"Just follow my footsteps in the snow; they'll lead you to my house in the forest," said Father Christmas. "Then I'll take your sack and sledge and go and knock on your door."

"Righto!" said the carpenter.

Then Father Christmas went to knock on Anderson's door, and the carpenter trudged through the snow in Father Christmas's footsteps. They led him into the forest, past two pine trees, a large boulder and a tree stump. There peeping out from behind the stump were three little faces with red caps on.

"He's here! He's here!" shouted the Christmas children as they scampered in front of him to a fallen tree, lying with its roots in the air. When Anderson followed them round to the other side of the roots he found Mother Christmas standing there waiting for him.

"Here he is, Mum! He's the carpenter Dad promised us! Look at him! Isn't he tall!" The children were all shouting at once.

"Now, now, children," said Mother Christmas. "Anybody would think you'd never seen a human being before."

"We've never seen a proper carpenter before!" shouted the children. "Come on in, Mr Carpenter!"

Pulling a branch aside, Mother Christmas led the way into the house. Anderson had to bend his long back double and crawl on his hands and knees. But once in, he found he could straighten up. The room had a mud floor, but it was very cosy, with tree stumps for chairs, and beds made of moss with covers of plaited grass. In the smallest bed lay the Christmas baby and in the far corner sat a very old Grandfather Christmas, his red cap nodding up and down.

"Have you got a knife? Did you bring some wood and some nails?" The children pulled at Anderson's sleeve and wanted to know everything at once.

"Now, children," said Mother Christmas, "let the carpenter sit down before you start pestering him."

"Has anyone come to see me?" croaked old Grandfather Christmas.

Mother Christmas shouted in his ear. "It's Anderson, the carpenter!" She explained that Grandfather was so old he never went out any more. "He'd be pleased if you would come over and shake hands with him."

So Anderson took the old man's hand, which was as hard as a piece of bark.

"Come and sit here, Mr Carpenter!" called the children.

The eldest one spoke first. "Do you know what I want you to make for me? A toboggan. Can you do that – a little one, I mean?"

"I'll try," said Anderson, and it didn't take long before he had a smart toboggan just ready to fly over the snow.

"Now it's my turn," said the little girl, who had pigtails sticking straight out from her head. "I want a doll's bed."

"Have you any dolls?" asked Anderson.

"No, but I borrow the field-mice sometimes, and I can play with baby squirrels as much as I like. They love being dolls. Please make me a doll's bed."

So the carpenter made her a doll's bed. Then he asked the smaller boy what he would like. But he was very shy and could only whisper, "Don't know."

"'Course he knows!" said his sister. "He said it just before you came. Go on, tell the carpenter."

"A top," whispered the little boy.

"That's easy," said the carpenter, and in no time at all he had made a top.

"And now you must make something for Mum!" said the children. Mother Christmas had been

watching, but all the time she held something behind her back.

"Shush, children, don't keep bothering the carpenter," she said.

"That's all right," said Anderson. "What would you like me to make?"

Mother Christmas brought out the thing she was holding; it was a wooden ladle, very worn, with a crack in it.

"Could you mend this for me, d'you think?" she asked.

"Hm, hm!" said Anderson, scratching his head with his carpenter's pencil. "I think I'd better make you a new one." And he quickly cut a new ladle for Mother Christmas. Then he found a long twisted root with a crook at one end and started stripping it with his knife. But although the children asked him and asked him he wouldn't tell them what it was going to be. When it was finished he held it up; it was a very distinguished-looking walking stick.

"Here you are, Grandpa!" he shouted to the old man, and handed him the stick. Then he gathered up all the chips and made a wonderful little bird with wings outspread to hang over the baby's cot.

"How pretty!" exclaimed Mother Christmas and all the children. "Thank the carpenter nicely now. We'll certainly never forget this Christmas Eve, will we?"

"Thank you, Mr Carpenter, thank you very much!" shouted the children.

Grandfather Christmas himself came stumping across the room leaning on his new stick. "It's grand!" he said. "It's just grand!"

There was the sound of feet stamping the snow off outside the door, and Anderson knew it was time for him to go. He said good-bye all round and wished them a Happy Christmas. Then he crawled through the narrow opening under the fallen tree. Father Christmas was waiting for him. He had the sledge and the empty sack with him.

"Thank you for your help, Anderson," he said. "What did the youngsters say when they saw you?"

"Oh, they seemed very pleased. Now they're just waiting for you to come home and see their new toys. How did you get on at my house? Was little Peter frightened of you?"

"Not a bit," said Father Christmas. "He thought it was you. 'Sit on Dadda's knee,' he kept saying."

"Well, I must go back to them," said Anderson, and said good-bye to Father Christmas.

When he got home, the first thing he said to the children was, "Can I see the presents you got from Father Christmas?"

But the children laughed. "Silly! You've seen them already – when you were Father Christmas; you unpacked them all for us!"

"What would you say if I told you I have been with Father Christmas's family all this time?"

But the children laughed again. "You wouldn't say anything so silly!" they said, and they didn't believe him. So the carpenter came to me and asked me to write down the story, which I did.

Alf Prøysen, translated by Marianne Helweg

If Santa Claus comes down the chimney

1　Here is a problem for you to expound,
　What is this rumour that's running around?
　Santa Claus comes down the chimney they say,
　Once ev'ry year giving presents away.

　　If Santa Claus comes down the chimney
　　After twelve at night,
　　Why doesn't he leave the soot
　　Where he puts his sooty foot?
　　Does he sweep the flue with his whiskers,
　　To make the fire burn bright
　　And if Santa Claus comes down the chimney,
　　What keeps his whiskers so white?

2　If Christmas Eve is his bathnight, I guess
　Santa must get in a terrible mess!
　Maybe each time he comes down from a flue
　He gives his whiskers a thorough shampoo.
　　If Santa Claus comes down the chimney . . .

3　Poor Missis Santa must certainly grouse
　If he leaves soot-marks all over the house,
　I think he must have some magical power
　Which turns the soot to the colour of flour.
　　If Santa Claus comes down the chimney . . .

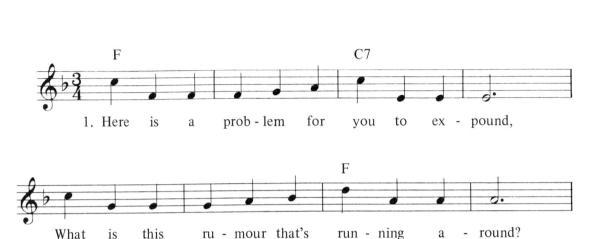

1. Here is a prob-lem for you to ex-pound,

What is this ru-mour that's run-ning a-round?

San - ta Claus comes down the chim-ney they say,

Chorus

Once ev - 'ry year, gi - ving pre-sents a - way. If

San - ta Claus comes down the chim - ney

Af - ter twelve at night,

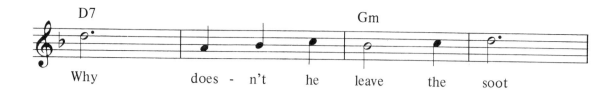

Why does - n't he leave the soot

Where he puts his soot - y foot? Does

- he sweep the flue with his whis - kers, To

make the fire burn bright _____ And if

San - ta Claus comes down the chim - ney,

What keeps his whis - kers so white? _____

John P. Long/Fred Gibson

When Santa Claus landed on the roof of the house with no chimney

It was Christmas Eve. When everyone was asleep Santa started to deliver the presents. It began very well until he came to the house with no chimney. 'Oh dear,' said Santa, 'there's no chimney. I must get my rope. Rudolph!' called Santa, 'will you give me my rope.' Santa got his rope and started to climb down to the bedrooms. He gave everyone a present and a card and then went away.

Aditi Keni, 8

Christmas characters 31

Up on the moon

Twas the night before Christmas, and up on
the moon
Not a martian was stirring; it was a little past
noon.
The stockings were hung in the crater with
care,
In the hopes that Santa would come right
there.
The moon kids were nestled all snug in their
beds,
And Mama in her craterchief and I in my
cap,
Had just settled down for a long moon nap,
When out on the moon dust arose such a
clatter,
I sprang from my bed to see what was the
matter.
But what to my martian eyes should appear,
But a tiny moon buggy and eight moondeer,
With a little old martian so lively and quick,
I knew in a moment it must be St. Nick.
And then in a second, I heard on the crater,
The stamping and stomping of hoofs grew
much greater.
As I was slowly turning and glancing around,
Down the crater chimney he came with a
bound.
He was dressed all in fur from his head to his
foot,
And his clothes were all covered with ashes
and soot;
A bundle of toys he had on his back,
And he looked like a pedlar just opening his
pack.
He spoke not a word, but went straight to his
work;
He filled all the stockings, then turned with a
jerk,
Putting his head gear over his nose,

And with a nod up the crater chimney he
rose;
He leaped to his moon buggy, to his
moondeer gave a whistle,
And away they flew just as fast as a missile.
But I heard on the intercom as he drove out
of sight,
"Merry Christmas to all and to all a Good
Night!"

Nona Maiola, 12
(after A Visit from St. Nicholas
by Clement Clarke Moore)

Dear Father Christmas

   I'm looking forward to your visit
on the 25th December this year. What
do you do when you have made your
deliveries to us? Which route do you
take from the North Pole to here?
I hope your reindeer are all right. Do
they ever play you up when you're in
the air? Have any of your reindeer
had a baby yet? Please could I have a
compass set and some pens and pencils.

   I do not want anything else,
thank you.

   Bye

   Jonathan

Jonathan Bairam, 10

Star-shaped Santa

The pentagon star idea on page 15 can be
developed to make a Santa figure. Count one
prong of the star as Santa's head, two more for
arms and the remaining two as legs. Use paint,
sticky paper, cotton wool etc. to decorate him on
both sides, and hang the figure on a thread.

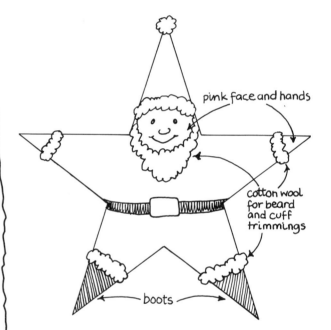

pink face and hands

cotton wool
for beard
and cuff
trimmings

boots

Knitted Father Christmas

This figure is based on the Teddy (page 95), but the pattern has been modified to accommodate more experienced knitters.

You will need:
Pair of No. 9 needles, 2oz (50gm) red double knitting wool, a small amount (less than 1oz) of beige (or light pink) double knitting, and the same amount of black double knitting wool. A sewing needle with a large eye, some white wool (or felt), and black felt scraps.

With red, cast on 20 stitches. Knit 42 rows.
Cast on 14 stitches at the beginning of the next 2 rows.
On these 48 stitches, knit 18 rows.
Cast off 14 stitches at the beginning of the next 2 rows. Break off wool.
Begin the next row with beige (or pink) wool and continue with this colour for 20 rows.
With right side facing break off the wool and re-join the red wool to knit hat section.
Knit 1 row.
Knit 2 stitches together at beginning and end of next and every 3rd row until 1 stitch remains.
Cast this off by breaking the wool and passing the end through the stitch.

Knit a second piece for the back.

Boots
With black wool, cast on 16 stitches and knit 10 rows.
Cast off 3 stitches at the beginning of the next 2 rows, then continuing on the remaining 10 stitches, knit 8 rows.
Then cast off.

Knit another piece for the second boot.

To make up
Place the two sides of the figure right sides together, and oversew all around the edge, leaving the bottom of the robe open. Turn inside out and stuff carefully beginning with the head.
Fold each boot in half and oversew around the edge leaving the top open. Do *not* turn these inside out, but stuff lightly.
Oversew along the bottom edge of the figure, incorporating the two boots.
Thread a sewing needle with red wool, and tie a knot in the end. Beginning at the neck edge, run a gathering thread around the neck-line, pull up slightly and secure with a few stitches.

Embroider eyes, nose and mouth.

The beard may be achieved in two ways.
(a) Use a double length of white wool threaded onto a sewing needle and sew the hair by making large loop stitches (secured by alternating with small close ones) all around the face. The beard stitches can be longer loops than the rest.
(b) Cut small pieces of white felt, appropriately shaped, and glue or sew them into place.

Additional decoration can be added to suit individual tastes. A belt can easily be fashioned from a strip of black felt or a length of twisted wool. Buttons can be sewn down the front. A cloak can be knitted (30 stitches x 48 rows), or cut from fabric, and secured with a drawstring.

A black felt sack would complete the outfit and could be used to carry a small gift to the recipient.

Father Christmas's Clothes

Joanna's cheeks were bright red with excitement. "Listen!" she called, "listen to this!" She rushed across the playground. "He's coming to stay with us. In our house!"

"Huh?" asked Sylvia. "Stay? Who?"

"Oh," cried Joanna, "Father Christmas, of course."

"Father Christmas?"

Now all the children were crowding round her. "Did you hear that? Father Christmas is coming to stay with Joanna."

"Ha ha! He can't. Father Christmas never stays with anyone." That was Billy.

"He must sleep somewhere, mustn't he?" That was Maria.

"But not in people's houses!"

"No. Where, then?"

"Father Christmas doesn't sleep. He rides over the roofs at night."

"Yes, well then he must sleep in the daytime."

"But not at Joanna's."

"Yes!" cried Joanna. "At our house. He's coming to stay with us. I saw it myself."

"Saw what? Father Christmas?"

"No," said Joanna, "his clothes." And she went on: "The bell rang and there was a man at the door. He had a big box. And Mummy said: 'Put it in the spare room.' But she wouldn't tell me what was inside. So I went to have a look, when she wasn't watching. The box wasn't shut and Father Christmas's clothes were inside it. I saw them."

The children stared, open-mouthed. But Billy said: "I don't believe it."

"Well," said Joanna, "you ask my Mum then." And they did. When school came out and Joanna's mother was standing at the gate waiting to pick up Joanna, all the children ran up to her.

"Mrs Green, Mrs Green, is it true, what Joanna says? That Father Christmas is coming to stay with you?"

Joanna's mother gave them an odd look. "How did you get that idea?" she asked.

"Ha ha! Joanna said that Father Christmas's box of clothes was brought to your house."

"Oh," said Joanna's mother. Her cheeks turned a little red, as well. "Yes, that is true. I didn't know you had seen that, Joanna."

Oh dear! Joanna's face was fiery red.

"Oh well," said her mother. "What you said about the box is true, but as to Father Christmas coming to stay with us . . . I don't know for sure."

"Oh?" cried Maria, "how funny. Then why would he have his clothes brought to your house?"

"Uhum," said Joanna's mother. She scratched her neck thoughtfully. "I think he must be coming, just for a day or two."

Then she took Joanna's hand and began to walk her quickly home.

The other children could see even from a distance that Joanna was getting into trouble – because she had given the secret away of course.

That night Joanna simply could not sleep. It's Christmas Eve the day after tomorrow, she thought. Father Christmas must have been travelling for a long time already and he will soon be here. But her mother had said that he would be much too busy to see Joanna.

"Father Christmas will only come home to sleep very late at night and he will have to be on his way again very early in the morning," her mother said.

I shall have to be awake earlier still, thought Joanna. And I shall creep very quietly to the spare room. In her mind she could see Father Christmas lying in bed with his beard over the sheet. In *her* house. Would he snore?

But it was already late when Joanna woke up and when she looked, the spare room bed was quite smooth. The covers were all straight. Could Father Christmas have made the bed up himself before he left?

"That must be it," said Sylvia, when Joanna told her about it. But Billy and the others did not believe it.

"He wasn't in your house at all," they said. "And he won't be coming, either."

Joanna was very upset and that evening in bed she pressed her face hard into the cushions to stop the tears, until she suddenly heard movements in the spare room. With a leap Joanna was out of bed. Could it be . . . She crept into the passage, listened at the spare room door and opened it very quietly.

She got a dreadful fright: there was Father Christmas! Father Christmas himself, in his red coat and with his red hood on his head. He was standing in front of the looking glass, combing his beard.

Joanna's mouth fell open. "Father__" she was about to gasp, but suddenly her arm was jerked, she was pulled back into the passage and the door was closed. It was her mother.

"Oh Joanna, you're not supposed to look. I mean: you mustn't disturb Father Christmas. You must stay in bed and sleep."

"Yes, but Mummy . . ."

It was no good. Joanna was tucked in again and soon afterwards she heard Father Christmas going out. Bang went the front door.

But I *did* see him, thought Joanna. I know he's true now and I know he's really staying with us.

"Ha, ha," cried Billy next morning. "I don't believe it. You're making it up."

"I'm not."

"You are."

"I'm not."

None of the children believed it except Sylvia, and of course she was Joanna's best friend. "Do you know what?" said Sylvia. "We'll come and pick you up to play tomorrow morning. It's Christmas Eve tomorrow and Father Christmas is sure to be there. He'll be having breakfast with you and we'll be able to see him for ourselves."

Sylvia always had good ideas.

But Mummy looked thoughtful. "I don't know if Father Christmas . . ." she began hesitantly, but suddenly Daddy said:

"I think he would. He'll need a good breakfast before he starts work, so he won't be leaving too early."

Joanna was so excited that it took her a long time to get to sleep that night and her mother had to call her three times next morning. "Father Christmas is having breakfast," her mother called.

Am I dreaming? thought Joanna.

When she came down to the dining room at last, Sylvia and Maria and Billy and Ann and Jeremy and Martin and Freddie were there and . . . at the table, calmly spreading his toast, was Father Christmas. He actually had a little egg caught on his beard.

"How late you are, Joanna," said Father Christmas. "Come and sit down quickly."

Joanna pinched herself to see if she was not dreaming after all. But Father Christmas was really there. He drank a cup of tea and ate another slice of toast and marmalade and all the children who had come, full of curiosity, to pick Joanna up, stood round watching him.

"Yes," said Father Christmas. "You wouldn't believe it, would you? But Joanna was right. She really had seen my box of clothes and where Father Christmas's clothes are, Father Christmas himself is not far away."

Paul Biegel, translated by Patricia Crampton

Good King Wenceslas

The popular carol, *Good King Wenceslas,* was written by the Reverend John Neale about a hundred years ago. The real Wenceslas was a Bohemian prince, not a king, who brought Christianity to his country. He was killed by his brother and his tomb became a famous shrine that was visited by many pilgrims.

Good King Wenceslas looked out
  On the feast of Stephen.
When the snow lay round about
  Deep and crisp and even.
Brightly shone the moon that night
  Though the frost was cruel
When a poor man came in sight
  Gath'ring winter fuel.

The tune dates from much earlier, and was originally not associated with Christmas at all, being a carol for springtime, with these words:

Spring has now unwrapped the flowers,
  Day is fast reviving,
Life in all her growing powers
  Towards the light is striving:
Gone the iron touch of cold,
  Winter time and frost time,
Seedlings, working through the mould,
  Now make up for lost time.

Christmas costumes

The standard costume

The 'T' pattern is an easily adaptable shape which requires the minimum of sewing skills. The costume requires only two seams, since the fabric fold falls at the shoulders. Use either 91, 114 or 137cm wide material and adapt the length to suit each individual child and the character he or she is playing. The neck openings can be faced with iron-on stiffening material (e.g. Vilene).

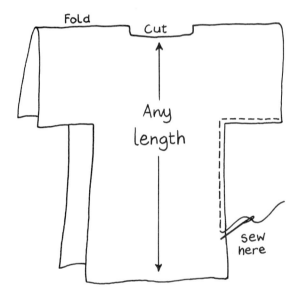

Angels

Wingless — Wings can cause more trouble than they are worth! Use the basic 'T' shape made out of white sheets, with tinsel for decoration — tied around the body, as headbands and even at the wrists. Angels can go barefoot or wear ballet shoes.

Shepherds

Interpret the basic shape in textured fabrics and dull muted shades; furnishing fabrics are a likely source as are old open-weave striped curtains. Use a variety of accessories: sling fur fabric diagonally across the body, cut an over-jerkin in contrasting cloth, bunch and wrap fabric over one shoulder. In each instance, the material used for the wrap-arounds and head-dresses should deliberately be left with raw edges to give a rustic, earthy look. Often a fine wool scarf with fringed edges or an old piece of thin blanket can be adapted for a head-dress, with fur fabric for the band; some shepherds may go bareheaded. Props include a staff made from a broom handle stained dark brown, shaped at the top with wire and bound with brown sticky tape; a shoulder bag; a toy lamb; and lanterns (you may find that an SOS will elicit metal lanterns — the paper variety may not stand the rigours of the dress rehearsal and performance).

Innkeepers

You can ring the changes with two different innkeeper costumes, both based on the 'T' shape. Again, use curtains or furnishing fabric of a lighter, silkier variety; even fine velvet can provide suitable material and complimentary wrap-around additions. Select richer looking cloth (brocade is perfect) for the cummerbunds and the wrap-arounds which can be attached with a brooch to the shoulder. Alternatively, choose an extra-long piece of fabric as a head-dress and shawl combined. With the layered version — a short 'T' tunic worn over an underskirt made from wrap-around cloth — no sewing is required; just firmly pin the skirt in place around the waist. Extras include leather neck purses or belts with purses attached, leather sandals and a variety of jewellery — bangles, chains, old necklaces.

Romans

Dress the Roman soldiers in a short 'T' tunic or cut one longer and hitch it up over a belt; choose plain fabrics (curtain lining quality is ideal) in bold red or yellow for the best effect. Over this, put a tunic made from black or brown felt stiffened with iron-on Vilene. Again, by folding the felt over the shoulder seams, there is no need for sewing; simply use a belt to keep the sides together. Cut the felt into shape and decorate with white felt marker or white paint and PVA glue. Wear with felt thongs tied above leather sandals, and also wrist bands cut from felt. Some children may be able to supply plastic swords (preferably a dark colour) to tuck into the belts, or make spears — again from broom handles — and staple on suitable card shapes in true Roman fashion.

Kings

For those who include the arrival of the wise men in their nativity production, here are a few ideas on royal attire! Again use the standard silhouette, cut from shiny, luxurious fabrics where these are available. Cloaks are essential, of course; old evening skirts make excellent cloaks, with brooches or fasteners, and fur fabrics or richly printed fabric trims. Here is your chance to go overboard with the jewels. Each of the kings can wear different crowns; one pointed, made from a cone of silver card – the brim in the same fabric as the costume, tucked and folded then decorated with jewels; another, a card band pointed at the front, decorated with sequins and then pushed firmly down over a large rectangle of plain fabric, caught underneath the cloak at the shoulders to achieve an Arabic effect; finally, a floppy chef's hat can be made from a scrap of green lurex, the card band decorated with fur fabric and then adorned with jewels.

There is another costume pattern fit for a king which could not be easier to make. Ideally, use furnishing fabric, which is the perfect weight and should be 114cm plus wide; you need to cut a length which is at least twice the height of the child. Fold it in half lengthwise; next, cut a slash in this fold to create an opening for the child's head to go through; edge with Vilene to prevent fraying. Fix two ties at waist level on the front of the costume (or use a belt if you prefer not to sew) and wrap this fabric securely round the body to form a long tunic. The remaining fabric at the back falls as a cloak; stick or sew on extra-wide furnishing braid around the cloak sides and at the hem; add fur fabric to make a collar if desired.

Sue Loveridge

Shepherds wake

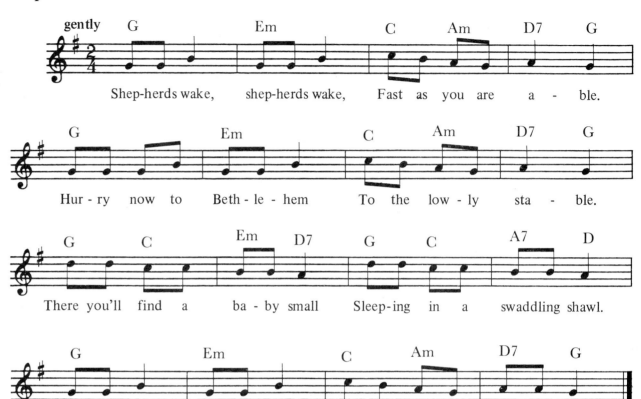

Shepherds wake, shepherds wake
Fast as you are able.
Hurry now to Bethlehem
To the lowly stable.
There you'll find a baby small
Sleeping in a swaddling shawl.
On your way, on your way,
See the baby born today.

music: Moravian carol tune
words: SN

This simple melody is ideal for beginner recorder players, and also sounds very effective over chords played on chime bars or metallophones.

Circular angel

To make the template, draw two concentric circles onto a piece of cardboard, for instance using a side plate and a yoghurt pot lid. Draw the head and arms, as shown, and give the wing edges a pattern.

Draw round the template onto white cartridge paper and cut out. Mark the two fold lines, then decorate the two different areas (wings and body) in contrasting ways on only ONE side of the shape, using any of the following ideas; gold and silver paint, gold and silver crayons, sequins, gold and silver foil, doilies, tissue paper, cotton wool etc.

Draw in the features. Fold the wings forward:

wings folded forward

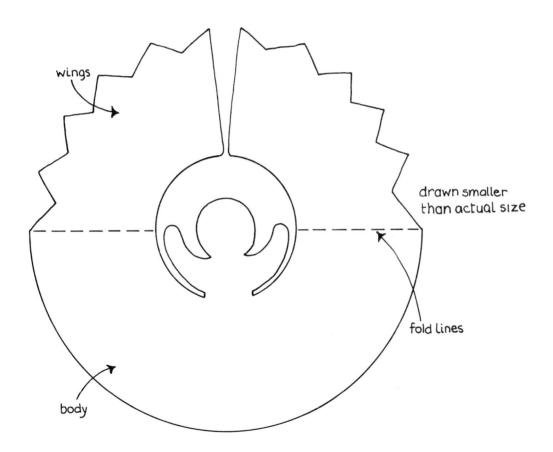

wings

body

drawn smaller than actual size

fold lines

Keeping the wings folded forward, overlap the two folds behind the angel and staple them firmly together where they cross over one another. The angel will then stand, or sit on a tree, or 'hosts' of them can be suspended by thread, e.g. from hoops.

wings folded back

Jelly case angel

You will need:

    a waxed jelly case with petal-shaped edging
    a small polystyrene or paper ball
    wool for hair
    a sequin
    a section of white paper doily
    glue, staples
    pens, paint, glitter

Cut the jelly case in half.

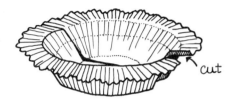

Roll one half into a cone and glue or staple down the overlapping edges.

For the head, make a small hole in the ball to fit the point of the cone, and stick it in place. Add lengths of wool for hair. Add arms made from sections of rolled paper doily.

Cut the other half of the jelly case in half again and stick or staple the two pieces to the angel's back – these are the wings.

Add a little glitter to the body and hair. Mark in the facial features and stick a sequin to the centre of the forehead.

Song suggestion

Band of Angels (*Count me in* 17)

Sir Oswald

It was a dark winter's night and Sir Oswald came home to his castle. He had come home a day earlier than anyone expected and so all the servants were away – doing their Christmas shopping. Sir Oswald opened the door and it gave a loud c-r-e-e-e-a-k . He felt for the candle and the matches. He lit the first match but the wind blew the flame out. He lit another match, but the wind blew this out too. Finally, he managed to light the candle with the third match, which was just as well, for there were only three matches in the box. The candlelight cast eerie shadows over the main hall of the castle, making Sir Oswald feel uneasy.

He decided to go straight to bed. As he started to climb the creaking stairs, he heard a noise from far off in the castle. RAP! RAP!...RAP! RAP!

It seemed to be coming from the other end of the corridor. He walked slowly past the bedrooms to the servants' part of the castle – at the end of the corridor. Now, Sir Oswald had never been in this part of the castle before. He heard the noise again. RAP! RAP!...RAP! RAP!

It seemed to be coming from a small door on the left. He opened the door and found that it led to a staircase that spiralled up and up.

'It must lead to the top of a turret,' thought Sir Oswald and, as he started to climb the stairs, he heard the noise again, only louder. RAP! RAP!...RAP! RAP!

Up and up the stairs he went, until he came to a door at the top. He opened it. The noise was much louder! RAP! RAP!...RAP! RAP!

He lifted the candle and shone the light around the room. It was empty except for a tall thin cupboard. RAP! RAP!...RAP! RAP!

The noise seemed to come from inside the cupboard. Sir Oswald walked towards it, opened the door...and there it was...a piece of *wrapping paper*!!! Then his candle went out.

Toni Arthur

Cardboard cylinder figures

These provide a simple but effective crib scene without the technical difficulties of making the figures stay upright.

You will need:
the inside cardboard tubes of toilet or paper rolls, scraps of material or wallpaper, wool, paint, paper and glue.

Stabilize the tube by sticking the bottom circular edge on to a piece of circular card 4cm wider than the diameter of the cardboard roll. When the glue has dried, drop a stone or lump of plasticine inside to give the figure extra weight.

Now cover the tube with fabric or wallpaper appropriate to the chosen character, add a paper face and top with woollen strands for hair, and a crown or head-dress. Arms are not essential but can be added by sticking one long strip of thin card (12cm long), covered on one side with the costume material, around the 'waist' of the model, leaving 3cm at each end free as shown.

Paper bag figures

These figures are ideal for the youngest children to tackle as they are very quick to make and require only basic materials.

You will need: paper bags (plain), newspaper, wool, fabric scraps.

Crumple enough newspaper to form a ball for the head and place it in the bottom of the bag. Give the bag a twist below the head and secure the neck with tied wool or a rubber band. The two corners of the bag which will stick out can be glued or sellotaped back to give a better rounded shape. Push a larger ball of crumpled newspaper into the remaining part of the bag to give support to the figure.

Draw on the features and lightly glue on wool for hair. Use fabric scraps for cloaks, robes and head-dresses, fixing them into place with dabs of glue. Paper plates cut in half can be stapled on for angels' wings, and gummed shapes may make suitable decoration.

Painting the figures is not recommended as over-wetting may cause them to collapse.

The Kings

Three kings from Persian lands afar
To Jordan follow the pointing star;
And this the quest of the travellers three,
Where the new born King of the Jews may be,
Full royal gifts they bear for the King;
Gold, incense, myrrh are their offering.

The star shines out with a steadfast ray;
The kings to Bethlehem make their way,
And there in worship they bend the knee,
As Mary's child in her lap they see;
Their royal gifts they show to the King,
Gold, incense, myrrh are their offering.

Thou child of man lo, to Bethlehem
The kings are travelling – travel with them!
The star of mercy, the star of grace,
Shall lead thy heart to its resting-place.
Gold, incense, myrrh thou canst not bring;
Offer thy heart to the infant King,
Offer thy heart!

Peter Cornelius, translated by H. N. Bate

Baboushka

An old Russian legend tells of an incident that happened during the Magi's journey to Bethlehem. The kings were following the star each night and then resting during the daylight hours. One morning they arrived at Baboushka's house, seeking lodging and refreshment. She was a hospitable woman and was pleased to offer them accommodation, but her curiosity led her to ask all kinds of questions and particularly why they chose to travel at night. When Baboushka heard about the new King she pleaded to be allowed to join the travellers, but insisted on tidying and clearing her house first. The kings agreed that she might join their party but told her that she must be ready by nightfall. Baboushka had not finished her tasks when the appointed time came and the kings left without her. When at last she was satisfied with her spotless house, she rushed to collect presents to take with her, and left, hoping to catch up with the kings.

The star by now had disappeared, so poor Baboushka reached Bethlehem long after Mary, Joseph and the child had fled to Egypt. Baboushka looks for them still, and each Christmas she leaves her home with her gifts. Whenever she passes a child's home, she hurries in, leaves a gift and then continues on her endless search.

Scrooge and his nephew

'A merry Christmas, Uncle! God save you!' cried a cheerful voice. It was the voice of Scrooge's nephew, who came upon him so quickly that this was the first intimation he had of his approach.

'Bah!' said Scrooge. 'Humbug!'

He had so heated himself with rapid walking in the fog and frost, this nephew of Scrooge's, that he was all in a glow; his face was ruddy and handsome; his eyes sparkled, and his breath smoked again.

'Christmas a humbug, Uncle!' said Scrooge's nephew. 'You don't mean that, I am sure.'

'I do,' said Scrooge. 'Merry Christmas! What right have you to be merry? What reason have you to be merry? You're poor enough.'

'Come, then,' returned the nephew gaily. 'What right have you to be dismal? What reason have you to be morose? You're rich enough.'

Scrooge having no better answer ready on the spur of the moment, said, 'Bah!' again: and followed it up with 'Humbug!'

'Don't be cross, Uncle,' said the nephew.

'What else can I be,' returned the uncle, 'when I live in such a world of fools as this? Merry Christmas! Out upon merry Christmas! What's Christmas time to you but a time for paying bills without money; a time for finding yourself a year older, but not an hour richer; a time for balancing your books and having every item in 'em through a round dozen of months presented dead against you? If I could work my will,' said Scrooge indignantly, 'every idiot who goes about with "Merry Christmas" on his lips should be boiled with his own pudding, and buried with a stake of holly through his heart. He should!'

'Uncle!' pleaded the nephew.

'Nephew!' returned the uncle sternly, 'keep Christmas in your own way, and let me keep it in mine.'

'Keep it!' repeated Scrooge's nephew. 'But you don't keep it.'

'Let me leave it alone, then,' said Scrooge. 'Much good may it do you! Much good it has ever done you!'

'There are many things from which I might have derived good, by which I have not profited, I dare say,' returned the nephew: 'Christmas among the rest. But I am sure I have always thought of Christmas time, when it has come round – apart from the veneration due to its sacred name and origin, if anything belonging to it can be apart from that – as a good time: a kind, forgiving, charitable, pleasant time: the only time I know of, in the long calendar of the year, when men and women seem by one consent to open their shut-up hearts freely, and to think of people below them as if they really were fellow passengers to the grave, and not another race of creatures bound on other journeys. And therefore, Uncle, though it has never put a scrap of gold or silver in my pocket, I believe that it *has* done me good, and *will* do me good; and I say, God bless it!'

from A Christmas Carol *by Charles Dickens*

T'is the season to be jolly

Customs and entertainments

Advent Calendar

Advent is the period of the Church's year that leads up to Christmas. Advent calendars that mark these days with doors or windows that open are sold everywhere and add to the children's anticipation and excitement. It can be difficult to make individual calendars that work satisfactorily, and the following idea for a corporate calendar offers a visually attractive and equally exciting alternative.

The school's most public area, be it vestibule or entrance hall, is organised to allow the mounting of one large picture per class. The subject of the pictures may be secular or sacred as required, and achieved through any medium favoured by the group or class undertaking them. The size of the pictures must be uniform to give the idea of the Advent Calendar 'windows'. Each class's work is mounted onto the display area but masked by two overlapping paper sheets acting as 'curtains'. These sheets may also be decorated.

During the last two weeks of term (or a time-scale appropriate to the number of classes) one picture is revealed each day by rolling back the 'curtains' and fixing them with paper-clips.

Marian Price

Christmas at School

Christmas at school begins in September when dates for carol evenings, plays, Christmas markets and parties are fixed with all the optimism and vigour that abounds after the summer holiday. Look into school three months later and you'll find teachers – knee-deep in paper chains, trimmings for party hats and the sparkling remains of spilt glitter and shredded tinsel – all questioning the sanity of trying to cram so many exciting events into the few short weeks that remain of the term.

However, such doubt somehow fades as events begin and the children breathe life into the rituals and customs of Christmas. School is a wonderful place to be at Christmas time. No matter how cynical or jaded adults have become about the commercialization of Christmas you only have to be around children at this time to realize it still has a special magic for them based on anticipation, imagination and participation. Anticipation – as the first door opens on the Advent Calendar and the countdown to 'the day' begins. Imagination – "I think Father Christmas will shrink and come under the door as we haven't got a chimney". Participation – that 100% of sheer enthusiasm that children put into all they do at this busy time of year.

Then watch the faces of parents as their child steps onto the stage to say its well-learnt lines, and listen to the voices of grandparents and other members of the community as they join the children in singing carols round the Christmas tree, and you know that through these children they are able to reach back into their store of happy childhood Christmas memories.

As days rush by and momentum gathers the bubble of excitement visibly swells until the last day of term arrives. After lots of noisy goodbyes and "Have a good Christmas" you retreat to a silent classroom to survey the remains of yet another year's festivities. December 25th is yet to come but Christmas in school is over. Away go the crib figures, tree and post box, and your thoughts can now turn to Christmas at home with your other family!

Marie Snape

We have come to Bethlehem

Miss Lee's infant class has prepared a ten-minute item for the Christmas Concert. Suitable costumes and props have been gathered for the occasion, the dialogue carefully rehearsed, and at 3 o'clock on the appointed afternoon the children and their somewhat harassed teacher are poised to perform.

Then Miss Lee stopped playing, and Rita put the light on and said to the visitors, "You sit there, you do. We're going to start."

The visitors sat down, all smiles and hats.

Then the light went out and Dick started 'While shepherds watched', very softly.

Harold got the bike lamps turned on. It was ever so pretty, Mary all blue and silver, and the sky and stars and the baby in the crib, the best baby doll in West Buildings.

Harold turned on the big star, and the shepherds came walking towards it, very slowly.

John Baker said, every so quietly, "Look, there's a shining star."

"We will follow the star," said Reg.

"And find the Holy Child," said Ray.

Then we all sang the second verse of 'While shepherds watched'. Chris dropped his wafer, but Mary was quick and she picked it up as the shepherd knelt down. Nobody saw, only me.

"Look, there's a shining star," said John Baker. Only he said it much louder this time.

Reg said, "You can't say that twice."

Miss Lee started playing 'Away in a manger'. Terry was singing.

The kings came out from behind the cupboard with their precious gifts. Jim had his mum's necklace on a cushion and Ron had some rubies, fruit gums really, and Depak had the box of blackboard chalk.

Then Ron stepped on the back of Jim's robe.

"Watch it!" said Jim.

Ron said, "We have brought precious gifts."

"You don't start, I do," said Jim.

"Well, get on with it," said Ron. "We haven't got all day."

"We have come to Bethlehem," said Jim.

"We have bought precious gifts," said Ron.

"For the Holy Child," said Depak.

Then he dropped his precious gift.

There was a crash and white dust and chalk everywhere.

from Eight days to Christmas *by Geraldine Kaye*

Christmas Eve

1. Ev - 'ry - bo - dy's wait - ing, Ev - 'ry - bo - dy's wait - ing, Christ - mas Eve,

Christ - mas Eve, Ting-ling with ex - cite - ment, Ting-ling with ex - cite - ment, Christ - mas Eve,

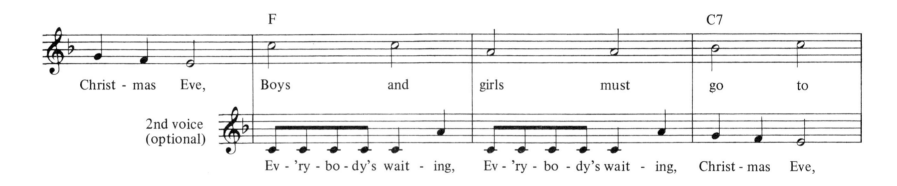

Christ - mas Eve, Boys and girls must go to

2nd voice (optional)

Ev - 'ry - bo - dy's wait - ing, Ev - 'ry - bo - dy's wait - ing, Christ - mas Eve,

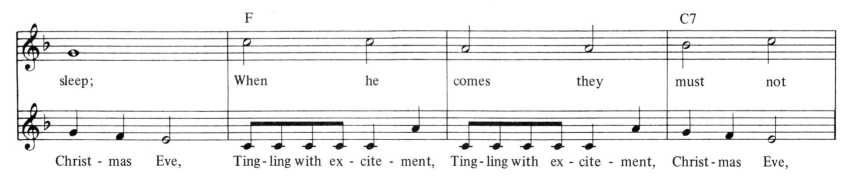

sleep; When he comes they must not

Christ - mas Eve, Ting-ling with ex - cite - ment, Ting-ling with ex - cite - ment, Christ - mas Eve,

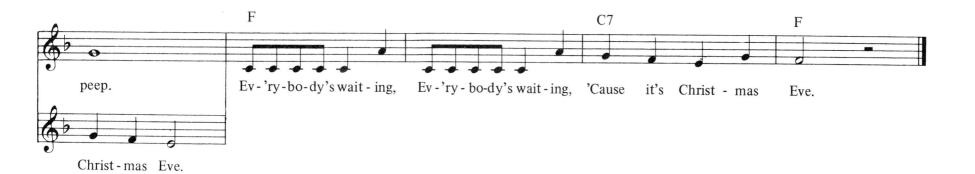

peep. Ev-'ry-bo-dy's wait-ing, Ev-'ry-bo-dy's wait-ing, 'Cause it's Christ-mas Eve.

Christ-mas Eve.

1 Ev'rybody's waiting, ev'rybody's waiting,
Christmas Eve, Christmas Eve,
Tingling with excitement, tingling with
excitement,
Christmas Eve, Christmas Eve,
  Boys and girls must go to sleep,
  When he comes they must not peep.
Ev'rybody's waiting, ev'rybody's waiting,
'Cause it's Christmas Eve.

2 Hanging up their stockings, hanging up
their stockings,
Christmas Eve, Christmas Eve,
Wonder what he's bringing, wonder what
he's bringing,
Christmas Eve, Christmas Eve,
  Boys and girls must go to sleep,
  When he comes they must not peep.
They'll be getting presents, they'll be
getting presents,
'Cause it's Christmas Eve.

3 Jesus in the manger, Jesus in the manger,
Christmas Day, Christmas Day,
Animals around him, animals around
him,
Christmas Day, Christmas Day,
  See the shepherds coming now,
  Wise men too before him bow.
Jesus in the manger, Jesus in the manger,
Born on Christmas Day.

Stuart Johnson

Suggested accompaniment for tuned percussion:

Perc I (tails up) uses low C and high C, plus F for last note
Perc II (tails down) uses low C, A and Bb, plus F for last note
last two bars:

Paul's Christmas Birthday

It was the middle of December. All the children in Paul's class were talking about Christmas.

Only Paul was thinking about birthdays at this time of year. Paul was thinking about birthdays because his was the day before Christmas.

"I hate having my birthday now," grumbled Paul. "What good is a birthday if everyone else only cares that it's Christmas?"

"When you were born, it was the nicest Christmas present I ever had," said his mother, who was cutting out dough for Christmas mince pies.

But this didn't make Paul feel any better. "I still wish my birthday wasn't now," he said.

Paul's mother smiled at him. She popped a still-warm biscuit in his mouth and said, "Cheer up! How about having a super birthday party? Your birthday may be only the day before Christmas for everyone else, but it's *your* birthday. And it's special."

In a few days, when Paul's friends came home from school, they found that the postman had brought them this invitation.

MEET SOMEONE FROM OUTER SPACE COME TO A SUPER BIRTHDAY PARTY THE DAY BEFORE CHRISTMAS 3.00 AT PAUL'S HOUSE

For the first time in weeks Paul's friends were taking about something besides Christmas. They wanted him to tell them who the man was from outer space. But Paul didn't know either. Everybody just couldn't wait for his birthday to come.

It snowed the day of the party. Paul kept running to the window to see if it had stopped. He had always wanted it to snow for Christmas, but he didn't want the storm to keep his friends from coming.

But nobody wanted to miss Paul's party. At three o'clock he heard boots stamping snow off on the porch. He ran to the door to let his first guests in. His party had begun.

The children hunted for hidden peanuts. They pinned the tail on the donkey. They had a contest to see who could keep his balloon up in the air the longest by just blowing on it.

Then they sang,

"HAPPY BIRTHDAY TO YOU.
HAPPY BIRTHDAY TO YOU.
HAPPY BIRTHDAY TO PAUL.
HAPPY BIRTHDAY TO YOU!"

And it was time to cut the cake.

But everyone was waiting for the man from outer space. What would he be like?

Suddenly there was a loud pounding on the door. Everyone looked at one another and giggled nervously. Paul's mother opened the door. A large man in a red suit stamped in.

"It's about time you let me in. It's cold out there!" roared the visitor.

"It's Santa Claus," one of the smaller boys shouted, jumping up and down.

"Santa Claus doesn't come from outer space," his older brother said.

"I most certainly did," Santa Claus said, straightening up very tall. "It's been a terrible day for flying, too. I got so many snowflakes in my eyes that I almost missed the house."

Everybody could see the snowflakes melting on Santa's lashes and on his beard.

"I brought a present for each of you," Santa Claus announced. "And since it's a special day today, you don't have to wait until Christmas to open it." He passed out small packages wrapped in birthday paper. "I have to leave now to get ready for tonight. But I didn't want to miss Paul's birthday."

"Happy birthday, Paul. Goodbye, everybody!" Santa called from the doorway.

When he left, the children looked outside to see where he went. But it was dark and all they could see were snowflakes.

Inside each package was a fuzzy animal hand puppet. The children were having such fun making the puppets talk, that when their mothers came to take them home, nobody wanted to leave.

At supper, Paul told his father about Santa's visit. "Do you think Santa will come to my party next year?"

"He probably will," his father said, "now that he knows when your birthday is."

Before he went to bed, Paul looked out of the window. The snow had stopped and the stars were out. Paul was too excited to sleep, but he wasn't thinking about his birthday any more. He was thinking about Christmas, because this year, at Paul's house, Santa was coming twice.

Carol Garrick

Let's make a party hat

Let's make a party hat,
Let's make a party hat,
Let's make a party hat
To wear on Christmas day.

1 First you cut a shape – snip snip snip,
First you cut a shape – snip snip snip,
First you cut a shape – snip snip snip,
Snip snip snip snip snip.
    Let's make a party hat . . .

2 Then you paint it ------- – slosh slosh slosh,
Then you paint it ------- – slosh slosh slosh,
Then you paint it ------- – slosh slosh slosh,
Slosh slosh slosh slosh slosh.
    Let's make a party hat . . .

3 Put on lots of ------- – stick stick stick,
Put on lots of ------- – stick stick stick,
Put on lots of ------- – stick stick stick,
Stick stick stick stick stick.
    Let's make a party hat . . .

Let the children suggest a colour for verse 2 and
a decoration (e.g. stars, ribbon) for verse 3.
They may also suggest suitable sounds (whether
sound-effects or untuned percussion) to
accompany the words *snip, slosh, stick*.

SN

Carols and Carol singing

The word *carol* may well have come from a Greek word meaning 'chorus', and the earliest carols of about 1300 were sung during ring-dances performed in the open. These songs blended pagan tunes and Christian words, but were sung in the vernacular, not Latin, a practice that met with severe disapproval from the Church. A more cultivated, refined form of carol also developed, especially in the 15th century, and this was probably used in ceremonial contexts, especially as processional music.

The folk-carols relied on peoples' memory for their survival and it was not until the 19th century that these carols were collected and notated for inclusion in hymn books alongside the more grandiose hymns of Wesley. During this time the tradition of carol singers collecting from door to door became established.

The current carol repertoire is enriched by new compositions and by the coming together of carols from many different nations. Many popular carols, however, still retain elements of the medieval 'dance-songs', sustained by an appealing, rhythmic, lilting tune, joyful, simple words and the common feature of a refrain after each verse.

First call: the Squire's house

Eight of us set out that night. There was Sixpence the Tanner, who had never sung in his life (he just worked his mouth in church); the brothers Horace and Boney, who were always fighting everybody and always getting the worst of it; Clergy Green, the preaching maniac; Walt the bully, and my two brothers. As we went down the lane other boys, from other villages, were already about the hills, bawling 'Kingwenslush', and shouting through keyholes 'Knock on the knocker! Ring at the Bell! Give us a penny for singing so well!' They weren't an approved charity as we were, the Choir; but competition was in the air.

Our first call as usual was the house of the Squire, and we trouped nervously down his drive. For light we had candles in marmalade-jars suspended on loops of string, and they threw pale gleams on the towering snowdrifts that stood on each side of the drive. A blizzard was blowing, but we were well wrapped up, with Army puttees on our legs, woollen hats on our heads, and several scarves around our ears.

As we approached the Big House across its white silent lawns, we too grew respectfully silent. The lake near by was stiff and black, the waterfall frozen and still. We arranged ourselves shuffling around the big front door, then knocked and announced the Choir.

A maid bore the tidings of our arrival away into the echoing distances of the house, and while we waited we cleared our throats noisily. Then she came back, and the door was left ajar for us, and we were bidden to begin. We brought no music, the carols were in our heads. 'Let's give 'em "Wild Shepherds",' said Jack. We began in confusion, plunging into a wreckage of keys, of different words and tempo; but we gathered our strength; he who sang loudest took the rest of us with him, and the carol took shape if not sweetness.

from Cider with Rosie *by Laurie Lee*

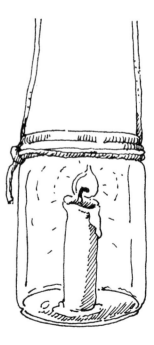

Carols at Mole End

Sounds were heard from the forecourt without – sounds like the scuffling of small feet in the gravel and a confused murmur of tiny voices, while broken sentences reached them – 'Now, all in a line – hold the lantern up a bit, Tommy – clear your throats first – no coughing after I say one, two three – Where's young Bill? – Here, come on, do, we're all a-waiting –'

'What's up?' inquired the Rat, pausing in his labours.

'I think it must be the field-mice,' replied the Mole, with a touch of pride in his manner. 'They go round carol-singing regularly at this time of the year. They're quite an institution in these parts. And they never pass me over – they come to Mole End last of all; and I used to give them hot drinks, and supper too sometimes, when I could afford it. It will be like old times to hear them again.'

'Let's have a look at them!' cried the Rat, jumping up and running to the door.

It was a pretty sight, and a seasonable one, that met their eyes when they flung the door open. In the forecourt, lit by the dim rays of a horn lantern, some eight or ten little field-mice stood in a semi-circle, red worsted comforters round their throats, their fore-paws thrust deep into their pockets, their feet jigging for warmth. With bright beady eyes they glanced shyly at each other, sniggering a little, sniffing and applying coat-sleeves a good deal. As the door opened, one of the elder ones that carried the lantern was just saying, 'Now then, one, two, three!' and forthwith their shrill little voices uprose on the air, singing one of the old time carols that their forefathers composed in fields that were fallow and held by frost, or when snow-bound in chimney corners, and handed down to be sung in the miry street to lamp-lit windows at Yule-time.

The voices ceased, the singers, bashful but

smiling, exchanged sidelong glances, and silence succeeded – but for a moment only. Then, from up above and far away, down the tunnel they had so lately travelled was borne to their ears in a faint musical hum the sound of distant bells ringing a joyful and clangorous peal.

'Very well sung, boys!' cried the Rat heartily. 'And now come along in, all of you, and warm yourselves by the fire, and have something hot!'

from The Wind in the Willows *by Kenneth Grahame*

Apple-howling

Wassail the trees that they may beare
You many a plum, and many a peare:
For more or less fruits they will bring,
As you do give the wassailing.

from Hesperides *by Robert Herrick*

Apple-howling was a Christmastide ceremony to encourage good cropping the following spring. "Howling-boys" are recorded as trooping through the orchards, chanting:
Stand fast, root, bear well, top
Pray the God send us a good howling crop.
Every twig, apples big,
Every bough, apples enou;
Hats full, caps full,
Full quarters, sacks full.

In one Somerset village there was a Twelfth Night gathering round the largest apple tree. The villagers fired guns to scare away evil spirits that might harm the crop, threw cider on to the trunk and placed cider-soaked cake on the boughs.

The Game of Popp

Mistress Prue to the spinette to play a merrie tune, and we to dancing once more stepping it right merrilie till Sarah do say its time for tea; whereon we do sit down and do justice to all the good things provided, which did make a brave show and looked verrie good on the dishes; the lights from the tapers in Johns mothers silver candle sticks did light the holly Sarah had put on the table in glasses. All the ladies did like mothers meat cake, and want to know how to make it.

Then we did gather together and play the game of Popp; we did put the chairs in a ringe, the men on one side, the ladies on the other with our hands behind, one holding a apple which be passed from one to another. The man must not speak but do beckon to the lady they think have got the apple; if she have not she do say 'popp' and the man do have to sit on the floor and pay forfitt, till all there; but if he be right he do take the ladie on his knees till the game be played out. After we did play bobbie apple, and snap draggon, the Passon burning his fingers mitilie to get Sarahs plum; all did enjoy it much, and then we did stop a while for sum cakes and wine, and sum songs sung by one and other; then more dancing till supper, then more games and later all home after a really good Christmas which we did all enjoy much with everybody happie.

from *Diary of a Farmer's Wife*

Our Hospital Christmas

Two weeks before Christmas the nursing staff put up the decorations around the ward and decorate the tree.

On the Maternity Wards a special fuss is made of the babies born on 25th December. Their cradles are specially decorated and reporters and photographers from the local papers come in and interview the mums and take photos of the Christmas arrivals. All the babies born during Christmas week receive small gifts which the nurses buy for them, which means that they have to organise special shopping trips when they're off-duty.

Local organisations send groups of carol-singers to bring seasonal music to the patients throughout the hospital, and the Mayor visits the wards and chats to as many people as he can.

Strict visiting times are dropped on Christmas Day and Boxing Day, and for this period it's open visiting which gives a much more relaxed and festive atmosphere.

Santa Claus comes to the Children's Wards distributing gifts to everyone, and so do the local football team which is a real treat for all the young sports enthusiasts.

The doctors and nurses rehearse a pantomime during the weeks leading up to Christmas. Patients are brought to the performance in wheelchairs, or on beds, for no-one likes to miss the hospital spectacular!

Christmas dinner is served on the wards with turkey, pudding and all the trimmings, and on that one day it's the consultants or senior nursing officers who carve and bring round the lunch to the patients.

Nobody would choose to spend Christmas being ill in hospital but everyone on the staff really tries hard to make it a happy and festive occasion.

Sister Mahes McKay

Crackers

The cracker, like many other Christmas customs, was popularized during the Victorian era. Tom Smith, a pastry cook, was visiting Paris when he noticed that a French confectioner was selling sugared almonds in paper twists. When he returned to England he copied this idea but added mottoes to the contents. An 1891 motto went:

The sweet crimson rose with its beautiful hue
Is not half so deep as my passion for you.
'Twill wither and fade, and no more will be seen
But whilst my heart lives you will still be its queen!

Here's a present day cracker riddle:
What do you get if you cross an elephant with a mouse?
Answer Great big holes in your skirting board.

The festive confectionary did not sell well until the invention of the exploding cardboard strip that gave the cracker its marvellous BANG!

Crackers were originally called *cossaques*. This probably refers to the Cossack marksmen, notorious for their haphazard shooting – the inevitable result of re-loading their rifles whilst galloping at full pelt!

Novelties were introduced later – these included head-dresses, masks, musical toys, perfume and fans.

One of the largest crackers ever made was constructed for a Victorian actor who was playing the part of a clown in a pantomime at the Drury Lane Theatre. It was 2m long and contained many tiny crackers to be thrown to the audience.

Song suggestion

Pull the cracker – BANG! (*Harlequin* 40)

Charades and word games

For many Victorian families, no Christmas Day was complete without a game of charades after dinner. Charades, which involves acting out words, was one of the most popular Victorian word games, enjoyed by adults and children alike. Other language games were more subdued; some were difficult, requiring the players to compose poetry; all provided fireside entertainment for children who, unlike their modern counterparts, were obliged to make their own amusement. Here are some of the more straightforward word games, suitable for use at home or in the classroom.

I love my love with an A . . .

This game starts with the letter 'A' and works its way through the alphabet. Each child has to provide enough words beginning with his allotted letter to complete the following:
'I love my love with an A because he/she is . . . (amiable).'
'I hate him/her with an A because he/she is . . . (awkward).'
'He took me to the sign of the . . . (Albatross) Inn.'
'And treated me to . . . (apples and artichokes).'
'His/her name is . . . (Alfred/Ann).'
'And he/she comes from . . . (Aberdeen).'
   A child who misses a word drops out of the game. In Victorian times, they would have had to pay a forfeit by doing something silly as a 'punishment', to amuse the other players. Recommended forfeits included counting from 20 backwards, and keeping a serious face for five minutes. Children today will enjoy making up their own forfeits. You may like to change the first line to 'I like my friend with an A . . .' to save blushes.

Alphabetical compliments

This is an easier version of 'I love my love . . .'. Again the game goes through the alphabet, and each child has to provide an adjective beginning with the allotted letter to complete the following:
'I like you, A, because you are . . . (amiable).'
'I like you, B, because you are . . . (beautiful).'
   You can modify the game to provide classroom practice with adverbs, e.g.:
'I like you, A, because you speak . . . (audaciously).'

Consequences

Give each child a pencil and paper. Each writes a boy's name at the top of the paper, folds it so that the name is hidden, and passes the paper to a neighbour. Everyone then writes 'met', followed by a girl's name, folds the paper and again passes it on. In the same way, the children write where the couple met, what he said, what she said, what the consequence was, and what the world said. All the folded papers are then piled up in a heap. Each child picks one out, unfolds it and reads out the story.

The secret word

One child leaves the room and the remaining children agree on a word. The child returns and asks each of the others, in turn, a question. Their answers must all contain the chosen word, but this must not be emphasised or made at all obvious. The questioner must try to work out from these answers what the secret word is. The child whose answer finally gives the game away leaves the room to become the next questioner. (Probably the best words for this game are common verbs, e.g. like, see.)

Cupid's coming

The children sit in a circle and choose a letter, e.g. 'w'. All the words used in reply to the questions that will be asked must begin with this letter and must end in '-ing'. The first child begins by saying to the second child, 'Cupid's coming'.
   The second child asks, 'How does he come?'
   The first child replies (if the chosen letter is 'w'), 'Walking'.
   The second child then says to the third child, 'Cupid's coming'.
   The third child asks, 'How does he come?'
   The second child replies 'Wandering'.
   The game continues in this way round the circle of children. Anyone who cannot think of a word is out of the game. A modern Christmassy version might be 'Father Christmas is coming'.

Dumb Crambo

Half the children leave the room, while those remaining choose a verb. When the other children return, they are given a word that rhymes with the chosen one. From this information, they have to try to guess the chosen word, but instead of saying what they think it is, they have to act out their guess in silence. If they guess correctly, they are applauded; if they fail, they are hissed. This goes on until the correct word is guessed.
   This game is popular with adults as well as children.

Charades

The children divide into two groups. One group leaves the room and chooses a word with two syllables, each of which makes sense by itself (e.g. playtime). They return to the room and act out the first syllable, then the second syllable, and finally the complete word. The other group has to guess from their performances what the word is.

Roberta Warman

Loop mobiles

You will need:
- various lengths of coloured card strips
- glue
- glitter
- sequins
- stapler

Take three strips of card of differing lengths — for example 50cm, 40cm and 30cm. Decorate each side with glitter or sequins. Staple or glue the ends of each strip together to form circles, then staple the three together as shown. Suspend the mobile with thread from the ceiling.

The card strips can be folded to create different shapes such as hearts or triangles.

Christmas across Europe

Each country has its own Christmas traditions that enhance the festive season. There is usually a jovial benefactor, like our Father Christmas, to bring gifts and foster a spirit of generosity and goodwill.

In Sweden, the festivities begin on St. Lucia's Day, December 13th. Young girls wearing white dresses and crowns of lighted candles lead processions through the streets, distributing coffee and cakes.

French children leave their shoes out to receive their presents from Père Noel. Beside the shoes they often leave a carrot for his donkey.

Spanish children also have gifts put in their shoes, but at Epiphany, for they believe it is the Magi who bring them as they make their way to the stable. The children sometimes sprinkle barley inside the shoes to feed the Kings' camels.

In Germany, dishes are left on the table so that the Christchild (Das Christkind) can leave nuts and sweets for the children.

An old woman called Befana brings gifts to the youngsters in Italy on the evening before Epiphany. She is supposed to bring gifts to good children, but those who have been wicked get only ashes!

The Polish tradition is to put hay under the table cloth and on the floor, to represent the scene at the stable.

The legend of St. Nicholas comes from Holland. There he is called Sinter Klaas. He saved three sisters from slavery and gave them each a sack of gold. These gifts started the tradition of present-giving to Dutch children on December 6th, his saint day. When Dutch settlers left for the United States they took their Christmas tradition with them, and their Sinter Klaas became the ubiquitous Santa Claus. St. Nicholas arrives each year by boat, wearing a long bishop's robe.

Boxing Day

St. Stephen's Day was traditionally the 26th of December, but this title became less common as the name Boxing Day was generally adopted. The 'boxes' may well have been alms-boxes placed in churches during the festive season; the money collected was then distributed to the poor and needy after Christmas. An alternative derivation comes from the earthenware boxes into which employers and customers put extra 'tips' for their servants. These were not smashed open until the holiday was over and the boxes were full.

Saturnalia

Each year in Rome, long before Christ was born, the people held a great winter festival called the Saturnalia. It was the time to pay homage to Saturn, the pagan Roman god of agriculture, whose name comes from the Latin word *serere*, to sow.

During this festival slaves were able to celebrate as equals with their masters, no criminals were punished and no wars were fought. The Saturnalia marked the beginning of the new farming year.

Epiphany and Twelfth Night

The final day of the Christmas period falls on January 6th and is called the Epiphany, which means the 'showing'. It celebrates the arrival of the three kings or wise men who came from the East, searching for the new Messiah. These royal visitors are traditionally given the names of Melchior, Caspar and Balthazar and their gifts were gold, frankincense and myrrh.

The Gathering round the Crib

Slowly and silently they came.
Before the manger with bent heads they
   bowed,
Having listened to the angels' voices ring
'Jesus Christ the Saviour, who is King'.
Three kings had come from far away
To see the new born King
In robes so bright and rich and bold
Bringing gifts of myrrh, frankincense and
   gold.
Next came the children, happy and gay,
Laughing and singing all the way.
They too, brought their gifts, precious and
   strange
Ball, boat, beads, Christmas rose and a half
   eaten orange.

10-year-old

The feast of Epiphany, also called Twelfth Night, marked the end of the Christmas holiday period, and there were many customs associated with this date. The Lord of Misrule ended his reign, and the traditional Bean Cake (see page 66) was served so that a king and queen might be selected to rule over the final night's revelry.

The Lord of Misrule

In the Middle Ages, on All-Hallows Eve, 31st October, the Lord of Misrule was selected. It was his task to produce continuous entertainment from New Years Eve until Twelfth Night.

The appointed "Lord" was usually someone of rather lowly status in the medieval court, and the revels that he organised would mock the loftier court members, creating an atmosphere of hilarity, with the conventional social hierarchy reversed.

The festivities would include pageants and masked dances with much music-making and feasting.

The practice of appointing a Lord of Misrule was forbidden by Cromwell, and was not re-introduced when the Puritan era ended.

Pantomimes

Pantomime originally meant acting "all in mime". It is the one extant remnant of the time when the Lord of Misrule reigned during medieval festivities. Then, the whole social order was upturned; in pantomime we now meet a girl playing the hero, or principal boy, and a man adopting the role of the Dame or Ugly Sister, while at the end of the play the poverty-stricken unfortunate wins fame and fortune and the rich powerful characters are overthrown.

Mummers

Mummer plays were common in English villages throughout medieval times. Each part was passed on orally from father to son, so that the role was usually kept within one family.

The players were always heavily disguised, for to recognise an actor's true identity was deemed unlucky. They wore masks and strange costumes made from rag-strips sewn on to old clothes. The villain represented Winter, and during the action he would slay the champion, Spring. A doctor would appear near the end and revive the hero.

The name mummers probably came from the German word *mumme* meaning a mask, though it has also been suggested that mummers are so called because the words spoken through their masks became an unintelligible mumble.

Christmas echo song
with vocal ostinato

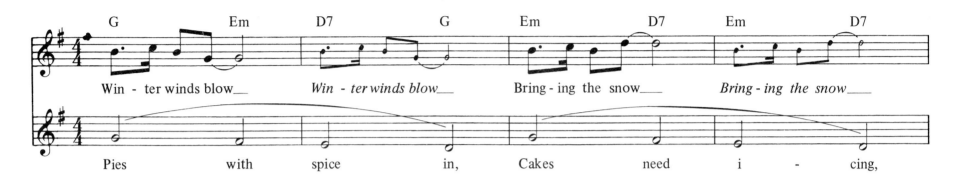

Win - ter winds blow___   *Win - ter winds blow___*   Bring - ing the snow___   *Bring - ing the snow___*

Pies   with   spice   in,   Cakes   need   i - cing,

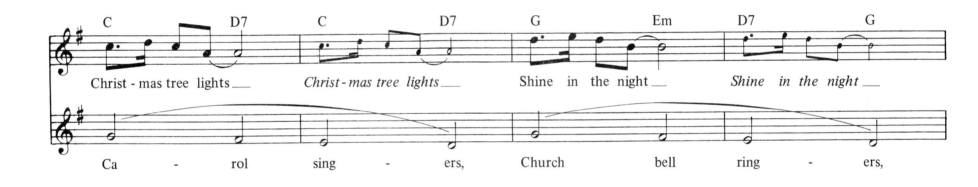

Christ - mas tree lights___   *Christ - mas tree lights___*   Shine in the night___   *Shine in the night___*

Ca - rol   sing - ers,   Church   bell   ring - ers,

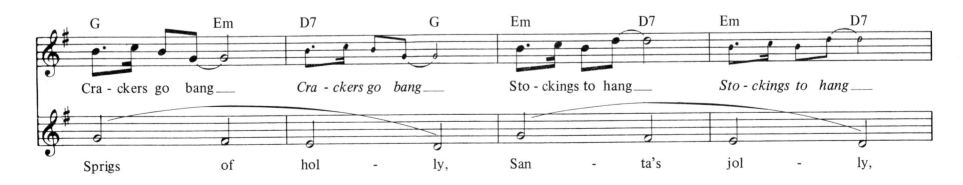

Cra - ckers go bang___   *Cra - ckers go bang___*   Sto - ckings to hang___   *Sto - ckings to hang___*

Sprigs   of   hol - ly,   San - ta's   jol - ly,

San - ta is due___ *San - ta is due___* Pre - sents for you___ *Pre - sents for you.___*

Red - nosed rein - deer, Christ - mas time is here.

Begin by teaching the vocal ostinato part, which may be supported by bass xylophones or recorders. Then teach the echo song in follow-my-leader fashion – teacher:echo for each phrase. Divide the group so that half sing the ostinato and the rest perform the echo song, initially with the teacher leading each phrase. Once the song is secure, a child (or small group) can lead the echo song.

Winter winds blow
Winter winds blow
Bringing the snow
Bringing the snow
Christmas tree lights
Christmas tree lights
Shine in the night
Shine in the night

Crackers go bang
Crackers go bang
Stockings to hang
Stockings to hang
Santa is due
Santa is due
Presents for you
Presents for you

Pies with spice in,

Cakes need icing,

Carol singers,

Church bell ringers,

Sprigs of holly,

Santa's jolly,

Red-nosed reindeer,

Christmas time is

Here.

SN

New Year's Eve

The arrival of the New Year has long been celebrated. In Scotland it is called Hogmanay and immediately after midnight had struck the famous 'first-footing' took place. People waited for a knock at their door before admitting a dark-haired man to step over their threshold. He brought with him tokens of good luck, such as coal, bread, money and mistletoe. These insured a prosperous year. Should, however, the visitor be lame, one-eyed or flat-footed, then bad luck would blight that household for the next twelve months.

In many cities and villages, church bells ring out the old year and welcome the new.

My New Year Resolutions

1. One of my New Year resolutions is to stop biting my nails. I MUST stop biting my nails. Because if I bite one of them too much then it starts to hurt and gets sore.

2. At the moment I am learning to play the drums. If I do not practise I won't get any better so I must remember to practise every day.

3. I must not be so horrid to my brothers although they get angry with me.

Richmond Stockwell, 10

Song suggestions

The miner's dream of home (*Okki-tokki-unga* 28)

New things to do (*Tinder-box* 58)

Our Chinese New Year

Our calendar is based on the moon, so dates are calculated from the previous new moon. Just as there is a leap year once every four years, we have a leap month every so often.

The Chinese New Year falls between the end of January through February depending on when the moon is next full. This is a time for joyous festivity and celebrating of old customs, which vary from family to family.

"It is bad luck to fight or argue," warns Mother. I think it's one of her superstitions to keep me and my sister from fighting. Other superstitions are never to sweep the floor during the time of festivity, nor to think badly of anyone, or cause injury.

On the eve of the New Year, my family dine together perhaps with cousins and friends. Special delicacies are prepared for this feast including dishes representing prosperity, happiness and a long life; for instance dumplings and mushrooms represent gold coins and bullion, noodles are for long life and cakes for happiness and promotion. My mother also prepares a fondue in which we can cook our own food. This meal takes at least two hours after which everyone is happy and full. A fish is traditionally left overnight signifying there will be plenty of wealth left for the family.

Throughout this festive time, lucky money given in red 'Lai see' packets is received by children. At home, my parents give me a lucky packet on the Eve, to be put under my pillow until the next day (rather like money from the 'tooth fairy'). Coins are placed on the ground overnight. On New Year's day, the first thing we do is to wish our parents "Kung Hai Fat Choy" (wishing you prosperity). The coins that were left overnight are picked up by my sister and myself in a race. I usually win but the money has to be shared out at the end.

During the day, we visit our elders – grandparents and great aunts etc. – wishing them a happy, prosperous long life and bringing them fruit and cakes. In return they give us red lucky money packets, and later on we are visited by others carrying the same message and trading red packets.

Our house is not greatly decorated, but trays or dishes of sweets, snacks and fruit are displayed.

Edwin Poon

We all want some figgy pudding

Christmas fare

Surprise Christmas Pud

This uncooked pudding looks uncannily like the traditional version but does not need endless hours of boiling in a steam-filled kitchen! The recipe is simple enough for children to follow and the finished 'pud' cuts very easily, providing at least 30 thin slices. Even dedicated chocolate-lovers will find this rich, and small portions are surprisingly filling.

Ingredients:
   400g mixed fruit
   4 tbsp orange juice
   100g glacé cherries (chopped)
   250g plain cooking chocolate
   100g margarine or butter
   150g digestive biscuits
   50g icing sugar

1. Soak the mixed fruit (but not the cherries) in the fruit juice for about 2 hours.
2. Break up the chocolate into squares and melt it with the margarine (butter) in a bowl over hot water, stirring constantly.
3. Break the biscuits into small pieces and place in a large bowl.
4. Pour the melted chocolate and margarine over the biscuit pieces and stir carefully to coat them.
5. Add the fruit, cherries and icing sugar and mix everything together well.
6. Line a 1½ or 2 pint (1 litre) basin with foil and spoon in the mixture pressing it down firmly.
7. Cover the basin with foil or clingfilm and put it into the fridge to set overnight.
8. To serve, simply peel off the foil and stand the pudding on a plate, and slice.
9. It will keep in the fridge for 3 to 4 weeks.

If a pudding shape is not critical, the mixture can be set in any other convenient mould, such as a loaf-tin or a deep cake-tin. It can then serve as a Surprise Christmas Cake!

The Robots' Christmas Dinner

When the Robots came to dinner
They came on Christmas Day
They wouldn't eat the turkey
They threw it all away
They ate up all the knives and forks,
and then they asked for more.
We've never had a Christmas Dinner
quite like that before!

Jan Holdstock

Christmas food song

Christmas pudding with brandy
  sauce,
Big roast turkey with stuffing of
  course,
Carrots and sprouts with roast potato,
Eat it all now and sleep it off later,
Jelly and trifle, Christmas cake,
All those things that Mummy makes –
Oh! dear! We nearly forgot,
Mince pies to finish with, nice and
  hot.

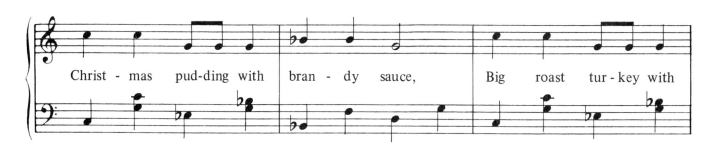

Eat it all now and sleep it off la - ter, Jel - ly and tri - fle,

Christ - mas cake, All those things that Mum - my makes____

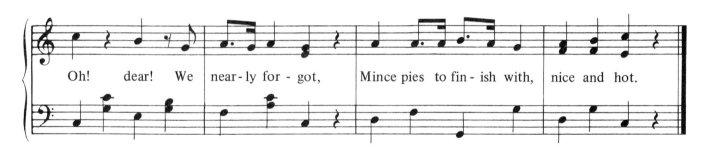

Oh! dear! We near-ly for - got, Mince pies to fin-ish with, nice and hot.

Stuart Johnson

The Christmas Dinner

At last the dishes were set on, and grace was said. It was succeeded by a breathless pause, as Mrs Cratchit, looking slowly all along the carving-knife, prepared to plunge it in the breast; but when she did, and when the long-expected gush of stuffing issued forth, one murmur of delight arose all round the board, and even Tiny Tim, excited by the two young Cratchits, beat on the table with the handle of his knife, and feebly cried Hurrah!

There never was such a goose. Bob said he didn't believe there ever was such a goose cooked. Its tenderness and flavour, size and cheapness, were the themes of universal admiration. Eked out by the apple sauce and mashed potatoes, it was a sufficient dinner for the whole family; indeed, as Mrs Cratchit said with great delight (surveying one small atom of a bone upon the dish), they hadn't ate it all at last! Yet everyone had had enough, and the youngest Cratchits, in particular, were steeped in sage and onion to the eyebrows! But now, the plates being changed by Miss Belinda, Mrs Cratchit left the room alone – too nervous to bear witnesses – to take the pudding up and bring it in.

Suppose it should not be done enough! Suppose it should break in turning out! Suppose somebody should have got over the wall of the back-yard, and stolen it, while they were merry with the goose – a supposition at which the two young Cratchits became livid! All sorts of horrors were supposed.

Halloa! A great deal of steam! The pudding was out of the copper. A smell like a washing-day! That was the cloth. A smell like an eating-house and a pastry-cook's next door to each other, with a laundress's next door to that! That was the pudding! In half a minute Mrs Cratchit entered – flushed, but smiling proudly – with the pudding, like a speckled cannon-ball, so hard and firm, blazing in half of half a quartern of ignited brandy, and bedight with Christmas holly stuck into the top.

Oh, a wonderful pudding! Bob Cratchit said, and calmly too, that he regarded it as the greatest success achieved by Mrs Cratchit since their marriage. Mrs Cratchit said that now the weight was off her mind, she would confess she had had her doubts about the quantity of flour. Everybody had something to say about it, but nobody said or thought it was at all a small pudding for a large family. It would have been flat heresy to do so. Any Cratchit would have blushed to hint at such a thing.

from A Christmas Carol *by Charles Dickens*

Diary of a farmer's wife

Dec. ye 23. We have bin verrie bussie with sum goodlie things to eat. Boiled hams and great big mince pies and roast geese and hens and boiled and roasted beef, all reddie for eating. Johns mother be going to make a pudden for carter and shepherd, and I shall give them a big mince pie and apples, so that they can have Christmas fare. Carters wiffe be cumming early to get ready for our visitors who be cumming tomorrow. We shall be verrie bussie, so I shall not have time to write in my book till all over.

Johns mother have made a verrie pretty dish wich she do call meat cake. She did mix flower and butter to a thick paste and put sum on the bottom of a bake tin, this she did cover with the chopt beef and onion and herbs, then more paste, then more meat and flavouring, and paste agen, till the tin be full. Then she do cover all with more paste and cook till done. She do say this do cut like a cake when it be cold with the meat inside. There be also 2 roast hares and pudden with spices and plenty of apple pies and divers things and junkets, cider cake and cinnamon cakes and a rich Christmas cake, Johns mother did bake.

I hope we shall have enough, but I be keeping sum rabbit pies and a big ham ready, in case it be wanted. John will tap the new beer and the honey wine, and we shall have primy rose wine, as well as Eldernberrie, and dandie lyon, so there should be good store.

End of Term

Let me begin with the Christmas treat at the school. It was always held on the day we broke up for the holidays. All pretence of work stopped at noon when we were set free for an hour's play in the open. It was the one time in the year when even a game of football could not hold our interest. Mothers and sisters had begun to arrive with exciting parcels. Our young bellies yearned for the spread to come. We made backs for each other – I was always the base – so that we might look through the windows, but they were so clouded with steam that we couldn't see anything.

Something happened at last to break the intolerable discipline of waiting. The school went mad. We left the shelters and porches, we deserted the doors and windows, we raised a communal yell of primitive delight and rushed about the playgrounds madly, pushing over the girls, trying to catch the snowflakes in our hands and even rolling on the ground in our ecstasies. The air filled with shrieks and yells and driven snow and the inhuman whistling of the wind. Suddenly the bell rang. The din halted for a moment of intense silence, for even the wind seemed to hold its breath. Then we all rushed for the schoolroom and the Feed.

The next four hours were the one time of the year when the school wore any aspect of true humanity. The sliding partition had been opened, throwing the two rooms into one, and revealing the total splendour of the decorations. It was a riot of coloured paper, evergreens and holly berries, and there was no contretemps, as on the occasion when one young devil adorned the portrait of Queen Victoria with turnip tops. The big table in the Infant room bore a noble array of tea-urns and cups, while another table supported a rare assortment of fancy cooking. Odd hampers stood about, full of luscious exciting things that would be

revealed in due course. It was with the greatest difficulty that we could be persuaded into our places. When we had been reduced to order, our mothers and sisters found seats on the benches where most of them had learned the ABC in their day; Miss Thom opened the piano; Miss Grey banged the floor with her pointer; and the company rose and burst into full-throated melody about 'When Humble Shepherds watched their flocks'. After the angels had been assumed back to Heaven, with a distressing uncertainty as to tone among the older boys, we chanted the Lord's Prayer with unusual heartiness and then broke

into a clatter of excitement. Two ladies appeared with the tea. Others distributed bags of cakes. The Grand Feed began. Each child received a bag of buns and a mutton-pie which had to be eaten before the more interesting sweets came round. We were not fastidious. Our rural appetites had not been corrupted by éclairs. We fell on the rather sober pastries with happy shouts and washed them down with cupfuls of hot sweet tea. It was a heartening sight, with sixty feeding as one, like a byreful of nought. When we had finished the plain fare and burst all the bags, after much misdirected expenditure of wind by the little girls, the mothers and sisters handed round their baskets of home bakeries – jam puffs, almond cakes, shortbread and sugared biscuits. And still the wonder grew that we didn't burst. Nature beat us at last. We had to give up.

from Farmer's Boy *by John R. Allan*

Christmas puddings

The first plum pudding was really a porridge and contained meat. Beef and veal were boiled together with wine, sherry and lemon juice. Dried fruit, sugar and spices were added, with brown bread to bind it together. The meat ingredients were gradually omitted and the pudding became a sweet course. Like Twelfth Night cake, the traditional pudding contained tokens which were usually silver coins. Sometimes a thimble and a ring were included, the latter to predict a forthcoming marriage.

> We wish you a Merry Christmas,
> We wish you a Merry Christmas,
> We wish you a Merry Christmas
> And a Happy New Year.
>
> Good tidings we bring
> To you and your kin;
> We wish you a Merry Christmas
> And a Happy New Year.
>
> Now bring us some figgy pudding
> Now bring us some figgy pudding
> Now bring us some figgy pudding
> And bring some out here.
>
> Good tidings we bring . . .
>
> For we all like figgy pudding
> For we all like figgy pudding
> For we all like figgy pudding
> So bring some out here.
>
> Good tidings we bring . . .
>
> And we won't go until we've got some
> And we won't go until we've got some
> And we won't go until we've got some
> So bring some out here.
>
> Good tidings we bring . . .

> Flour of England, fruit of Spain,
> Met together in a shower of rain;
> Put in a bag, tied round with a string;
> If you tell me this riddle,
> I'll give you a ring.

> Charlie Wag,
> Charlie Wag,
> Ate the pudding
> And left the bag.

St. Nicholas letter biscuits

Ingredients:
  400g pastry
  200g marzipan
  milk

1. Set the oven to 425° F, 218° C or gas mark 7.
2. Roll out the pastry on a floured surface and cut into strips 4cm wide and 10cm long.
3. Knead the marzipan to soften it and take small pieces one at a time, rolling them into thin 'sausages' roughly 1cm in diameter.
4. Trim each 'sausage' to fit to a pastry strip. Seal the long pastry edges around the marzipan with milk and push into letter shapes. Complicated letters may require longer strips, so join two together with milk.
5. Place the letters on a greased baking sheet and bake for 10 minutes.
6. Cool on a wire rack.

Instead of little letters, one large initial (representing the first letter of your family's surname) can be made. For this, roll the pastry into one large strip approx. 10cm wide and 25cm long.

The Dutch celebrate the festive side of Christmas on the feast of St. Nicholas, December 6th. Traditionally, all sorts of confectionary in the form of letters are exchanged as gifts at this time of year. These letter biscuits – called *Boterletters* in Holland – are usually made in the home, but chocolate letters and other biscuits are also available in the shops. The same recipe is used for a *Kerstkrans* – A Christmas wreath – eaten on Christmas Day itself. The pastry and almond strip is formed into a circle and decorated with icing sugar and cherries.

Of course, naughty children do not receive anything. 'Zwarte Piet' – Black Pete – follows St. Nicholas, and children who have not been good risk being carried off by him!

Marie Lou Vanderburg

Meat

Many different kinds of meat have been offered at the Christmas table, and our modern Christmas dinners seem a mere shadow when compared with the lavish feasts of Christmas past! King Henry V served a wide range of fish at his table, including sturgeon, porpoise and eels. Fifteenth-century banquets included herons, swan, quail, egret and peacock. The latter was often presented with its plumage replaced and a gilded beak. These feasts would not have been complete without the boar's head which was brought to the table on a platter, with an orange or an apple in its mouth. This ceremony survives still at Queen's College, Oxford.

> . . . send up the Brawner's Head,
> Sweet Rosemary and Bays around it spread.
> His foaming tusks let some large pippin grace,
> Or 'midst these thundering spears an orange place.

from Art of Cookery *by William King (17th century)*

Frumenty

This was an Anglo-Saxon dish rather like a thick sauce, made by boiling milk with wheat, and sometimes sweetened with honey. It was eaten as a breakfast on Christmas morning or served as an accompaniment to meat dishes. Frumenty remained a popular dish until the end of the 19th century.

Mince pies

These, like the puddings, were originally baked with meat. Typical ingredients were pheasant, hare, pigeon, rabbit, mushrooms, eggs and seasoning. The traditional shape was oblong, to represent the crib, and was surmounted by a pastry figure of Christ. Oliver Cromwell prohibited these pies as pagan frivolities, but when Christmas festivities returned (with the restoration of Charles II) there were no longer pastry figures and the shape had become round.

Folklore states that the daily eating of a mince pie from Christmas Day until Twelfth Night would guarantee the eater a prosperous year. The famous pie eaten by Jack Horner in the nursery rhyme was a gift from a somewhat nervous Abbot of Glastonbury to his monarch. Deeply worried by the threat of confiscation of his lands, the Abbot entrusted the pie to Jack Horner, his squire. During the journey the young man discovered some title deeds beneath the pastry, obviously intended to sway the king's resolve. Horner appropriated the deeds and later took possession of the property.

Christmas Eve

Christmas Eve was crisp and cold and bright and we were going carol singing in the evening, so that I wanted to have mince-pies and sausage rolls ready to contribute to what we would all scoff afterwards. The kitchen was smelling wonderfully aromatic, of warm pastry and brandy and mincemeat, and it was very hot, too. Jessica seemed oddly subdued and a little flushed, as she rolled her own piece of shortcrust pastry to within an inch of its life, but then, so was I flushed, and I didn't take much notice. The first batch of pies was cooling on the wire rack when the window-cleaners arrived – not a pair of them, as usual, but four, and wanted some milk for their tea, and gazed at the mince-pies like hungry schoolboys until I offered them and they took two each, so I had to start on more pastry. Then a friend from the other side of the village brought a Christmas fruit loaf dusted with icing sugar and tied in yellow ribbon and a cloth, and told us her goat had got out and if we saw it . . . and then another neighbour with two small sons and a party invitation arrived and the kettle went on and more pies disappeared and the kitchen was packed with happy people and Jessica was looking even more flushed, and I was thinking of bringing out the plum brandy and turning the whole thing into a party when a window-cleaner shouted through an opened window that there was a man outside with a crateful of hens. And so there was, our hens had arrived in time for Christmas, and everyone came out to look and admire their creamy whiteness and see them installed in the hen house, and suddenly the hall was full of sacks of layers' mash and corn and a bale of straw and over the wireless came the first of the Nine Lessons and Carols from King's College, Cambridge.

By the time everyone had left, nearly two dozen of the mince-pies and a lot of sausage rolls had been consumed and there were none for us or the carol singers. I heaved another bag of flour out of the larder and Jessica went off to watch 'Play School' and fell asleep over it, still oddly flushed. By the time I set off for the church in my scarf and boots, I never wanted to see another spoonful of mincemeat, and there was a goat in the garden.

The next morning, we woke early, to the sound of the bells pealing Christmas through the village. It was another golden day, of frosty cold and brilliant sunshine. A hen had laid one egg for Christmas and Jessica was entirely covered in little pink spots.

from The Magic Apple Tree *by Susan Hill*

Mince pie calypso

1 Christmas was a week away,
   I went out to tea.
  It was Granny's baking day
    And she gave me mince pies,
     one, two, three.

    I ate them all, and I'll tell you
      why;
    You get a happy month for
      each mince pie.
    I'm sure to be happy for years
      and years
    Now I've got mince pies
      coming
    Out of my ears.

2 Next day when my Auntie came,
   She'd a nice surprise.
  In a great big shiny tin
    There were lots and lots of hot
     mince pies!
     I ate them all, and I'll tell you
     why . . .

3 There was nothing left for tea
   On the larder shelf,
  So I thought I'd have a go,
    And I made some more mince
     pies myself!
     I ate them all, and I'll tell you
     why . . .

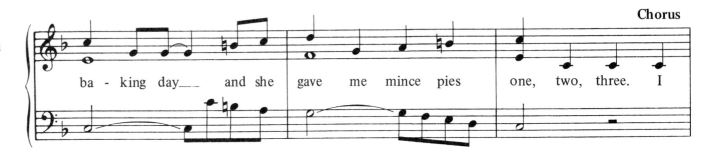

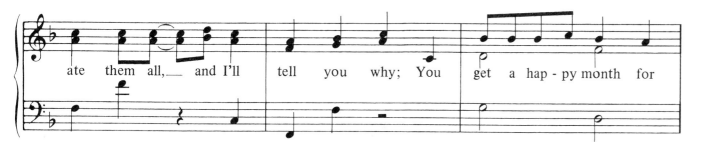

ate them all,___ and I'll | tell you why; You | get a hap-py month for

each mince pie. I'm | sure to be hap-py for | years and years now I've got

mince pies com-ing | out of my ears.___

Jan Holdstock

Mincemeat slices

This is a wholefood alternative to the traditional mince pies.

Ingredients:
  150 g margarine
   75 g soft brown sugar
  225 g wholewheat flour
  110 g porridge oats
  a generous $\frac{1}{2}$lb (225 g) of mincemeat

Set the oven to 400°F, 200°C or gas mark 6.
You will need a shallow baking tin, 11″ × 7″, buttered or lined with non-stick baking parchment.

1. Melt the margarine and sugar in a large saucepan.
2. Mix the flour and oats together in a mixing bowl.
3. Remove the saucepan from the heat and stir in the flour and oats, blending thoroughly.
4. Spoon half of the mixture into the baking tin, pressing firmly down especially into the corners.
5. Spread the mincemeat over the top, and then the remaining oat mixture on top of that, again pressing down firmly.
6. Cook in the centre of the oven for about 20 minutes or until the top is tinged brown.
7. Remove from the oven and cut into squares or slices, but leave in the tin until cold. Store in an airtight tin.

Ostinato for scraper:

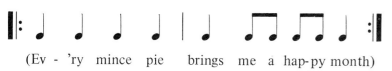

(Ev - 'ry mince pie brings me a hap-py month)

Bean Cake

In medieval times, Twelfth Night Cake, or Bean Cake, was cooked to celebrate the coming of the three Kings at Epiphany. A bean and a pea were added to the mixture before baking, and the finished cake was iced and ornately decorated with stars and images of the Kings. The man who found the bean, or the woman who found the pea, would be King and Queen for the last night of the Lord of Misrule's reign (see page 53). Should a man find the pea he could choose his Queen, and similarly a woman finding the bean was entitled to select her King.

> Now, now the mirth comes
> With the cake full of plums,
> Where Beane's the King of the sport here;
> Beside we must know,
> The Pea also
> Must revell, as Queene, in the court here.
>
> Begin then to chuse,
> (This night as ye use)
> Who shall for the present delight here,
> Be a King by the lot,
> And who shall not
> Be Twelfe-day Queen for the night here.

from Twelfe Night *by Robert Herrick*

At one King's court a pie, not a cake, was presented, and to the amazement of the company from under the pie-crust flew singing birds. This surely must explain the rhyme 'Sing a song of sixpence'.

The ceremony of the bean cake has given us the expression 'a beanfeast'.

Stir-up Sunday

The last Sunday before Advent was traditionally known as Stir-up Sunday, and was regarded as the last opportunity for making Christmas puddings. The 'stir-up' does not refer to the mixing of ingredients, but rather derives from the opening line of that Sunday's collect, "Stir up, we beseech Thee, O Lord, the wills of thy faithful people . . ." Each member of the family stirred the mixture and made their wish.

Dumb cakes

This was a custom practised on Christmas Eve, when each unmarried girl would make a 'dumb cake'. The entire preparation was undertaken in silence, until at midnight, according to legend, the girl's future husband would appear at the door. In a Cotswolds variation of this tradition, the girl would mark her initials on the cake and at twelve o'clock her suitor would enter the kitchen, open the oven and add his initials to the cake.

Snapdragon

Snapdragon was a game for Christmas Eve. Dried fruits such as raisins and currants were placed in a bowl, and brandy was poured over the top. As this was ignited, the lights were put out and the participants had to snatch the fruit and eat it.

> Here he comes with flaming bowl,
> Don't be mean to take his toll,
> Snip! Snap! Dragon!
>
> Take care you don't take too much,
> Be not greedy in your clutch,
> Snip! Snap! Dragon!
>
> With his blue and lapping tongue
> Many of you will be stung,
> Snip! Snap! Dragon!
>
> For he snaps at all that comes
> Snatching at his feast of plums,
> Snip! Snap! Dragon!
>
> But Old Christmas makes him come,
> Though he looks so fee! fa! fum!
> Snip! Snap! Dragon!
>
> Don't 'ee fear him, be but bold –
> Out he goes, his flames are cold.
> Snip! Snap! Dragon!

More songs to sing

The Gloucestershire Wassail (*Merrily to Bethlehem* 44)

The Wassail of Figgy Duff (*Merrily to Bethlehem* 43)

Christmas Cake (*Flying a Round* 61)

Robin's ruddy tum

Animals and birds

Circular robins

These robins are effective, simple and quick to produce. Large double-sided ones make excellent mobiles; smaller ones stuck onto folded cartridge paper make attractive Christmas cards, and tiny ones can be used as gift tags or tree decorations.

You will need:
a plate, saucer or circular template of the size you require and any of the following materials in brown or red — paint, sticky paper, shiny paper, fabric, tissue or crêpe paper.

Draw round your circle on to thin card. Before cutting out draw a beak and a pair of *simple* legs (don't bother with claws; they are difficult to cut out). Draw a line that approximately halves the circle, then cut out your robin. Decorate the top brown and the breast red in any way that suits the capabilities of the children involved.

Very young children will cope easily with tearing and sticking tissue paper or pre-cut fabric pieces, whereas older, more dextrous children will enjoy

designing more complicated decorations. For example, cut plenty of small triangles (use 'tall' isosceles triangles rather than equilateral ones) and fold a small strip along the shortest side.

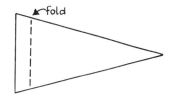

fold

Beginning at the 'back' of the robin, i.e. the edge furthest from the beak, stick each triangle down by its folded strip. Work in layers towards the beak to achieve a feathery effect. The beak and legs can be painted yellow, and a sequin makes a twinkling eye.

Marian Price

The Robin

The robin, with its familiar red breast (found on male and female alike), is one of the best-loved of birds, and its popularity as a Christmas card subject never seems to wane.

The robin's song is one of the first to be heard in the dawn-chorus. It sings to warn the other robins to keep away from its territory, and puffs itself up to seem more intimidating.

Many countries know the robin as a seasonal visitor, but in the British Isles it is more often a permanent resident. It is among the tamest of garden birds, often hopping boldly to within a few feet of where a gardener is working.

Robin's Song

Robin sang sweetly
    When the days were bright.
'Thanks! Thanks for Summer!'
    He sang with all his might.

Robin sang sweetly
    In the Autumn days:
'There are fruits for everyone.
    Let us all give praise!'

In the cold and wintry weather
    Still you hear his song.
'Somebody must sing,' said Robin,
    'Or Winter will seem long.'

When the Spring came back again,
    He sang, 'I told you so!
Keep on singing through the Winter;
    It will always go.'

Anon.

Robin Redbreast

1 Robin Redbreast in the doorway,
   Fixed his beady eyes upon me,
   Cocked his little head so quaintly,
   "It is cold: the snow is coming."

2 Robin raised his head toward me:
   "Have you crumbs of bread to feed me,
   And a nest where you can hide me?
   It is cold: the snow is coming."

3 "I will build a nest to hide thee;
   Through the winter I will feed thee."
   Robin spread his wings and thanked me:
   "It is cold: the snow is coming."

anon.

The White Robin

On the very last day of the holidays the early sunshine woke me. I sat up in bed, and looked into the branches of an ancient apple tree outside the bedroom window.

There, its tiny talons gripping a lichen-covered twig, sat the white robin. Its eyes were dark and shining against the white satin of its head. The breast was still more orange than red, and glowed against its snowy plumage.

It was a breath-taking sight, and I did not dare to move. For a full half minute it sat there motionless, and then with a flash of white wings, it had gone.

At much the same time, whilst I was reading that delightful book *The Country Diary of An Edwardian Lady,* I discovered that one of the January entries mentions 'a very curious Robin' which the author describes as a light silvery grey and looking like a white bird with a scarlet breast when in flight.

As the weather grew colder, more and more birds sought out the scraps provided, both on my garden bird table and in the playground. They seemed to come in groups. A blue-tit would appear, followed by half a dozen more. Then the chaffinches would sense that here was food to be had, and the blackbirds and always, of course, the ubiquitous sparrows and starlings.

They would make a concerted rush upon the food available, and then something would startle them and the bird table would be empty in a flash of wings. It was after just such a sudden exodus when I was turning away from the window that the white robin came again.

With his matchstick legs askew, and his liquid dark eyes cocked upon the bounty, he was poised there for a full minute pecking at the scraps which he now enjoyed alone. His orange breast glowed like embers against the snowy feathers. He was even more handsome than on his first appearance.

Miss Read

The Redbreast

The redbreast smoulders in the waste of
   snow:
His eye is large and bright, to and fro
He draws and draws his slender threads
   of sound
Between the dark boughs and the freezing
   ground.

Anthony Rye

Riddle

"I'm called by the name of a man,
Yet am as little as a mouse;
When Winter comes I love to be
With my red target near the house."

The Brave Robin

One cold snowy winter when all the birds were hungry, a robin and his mate discovered a regular supply of crumbs put out by some thoughtful children on their nursery window-sill.

As the two birds feasted on Christmas cake crumbs, they saw the family's glittering Christmas tree through the window. Mrs Robin begged her husband to take a few strands of tinsel to decorate her nest for next Spring, and Bob, the cock-robin, eventually agreed to get his wife some 'silver moss' (as she called it) from the tree.

Bob looked at the window, it was open a tiny bit at the top, and he saw that the room was empty. He flew up and through the window, alighting on the top of a low cupboard.

Turning his head to look at the Christmas tree, he was almost startled out of his wits! Close to him was a great open mouth, with enormous teeth, and two eyes glared at him fiercely. Bob thought some awful creature was ready to eat him up, he didn't know it was only a rocking horse.

He flew in a great fright to a chair on the other side of the room, but scarcely had he reached it when he was off again, this time to the top of the window curtains, where he sat trembling. Sitting on the chair was a large doll. She had fair hair and big blue eyes, and those eyes had been looking straight at Bob. And now, as he looked round the room, he saw other eyes watching him. On the floor lay a teddy bear staring up at him severely, and in the corner a wooden soldier stood pointing his gun at him.

"Bless me!" Mr. Robin said to himself. "What am I to do?" He looked down into the room again, and then he understood – they were only toys after all, and no more alive than were the tiny ones on the Christmas tree. He sighed a great sigh of relief, then flew down, and sitting on the doll's chair, he pulled her hair. Next he pecked the teddy bear's nose, but he left the rocking horse alone, and went off to the Christmas tree.

The tinsel shone, and the glass balls twinkled in the firelight, and the tiny toys looked at him with tiny eyes.

Bob was very busy trying to find the best and shiniest piece of tinsel for his wife, when he almost jumped out of his skin! The door opened suddenly, and children and grown-ups crowded into the room. The window was closed, the curtains were drawn, and the children skipped and jumped round the tree, telling one another how lovely it was, and clamouring for the candles to be lighted. Bob was too terrified to move.

He cowered there against the slim trunk of the tree, gazing dumbly through the branches at the people round him, hoping and hoping that he wouldn't be seen. And then he felt more scared than ever, for a tall man began to light the candles. The children laughed and chattered, but Bob crouched lower and lower, wondering how soon his feathers would be singed.

Soon the children danced round the tree, singing as they went, and then the tall man called out, "Now for the presents!" The first little girl chose a blue and green rubber ball, and the little boy chose an engine. The third, a very tiny girl, asked

shyly for the fairy doll at the top of the tree, and the tall man stood on a chair to reach it down for her.

And then Bob heard the next child say, "Please may I have the toy robin?" And his little heart nearly stopped beating.

"Toy robin?" asked the tall man, "but I don't think there is one on the tree!"

"Yes there is," said the child in a surprised voice – "Look!" and then she pointed her finger straight at Bob, and everyone looked up at him. "So there is," the tall man said, "I wonder how it got there?" And he went round to the other side of the tree to get the chair to stand on.

Bob shook so much with fright that he thought he would fall off the tree. If he didn't do something quickly he would be kept here as a toy robin – in this nursery with the staring doll and the dreadful horse. What could he do? His head was in a whirl . . .

And then suddenly, he knew. The very wisest thing he could do was to show all these people that he was a real, live robin, and not a silly toy.

He stopped trembling, and with fluttering wings he sprang to the topmost branch of the tree. There he threw back his head, opened his little beak, and sang and sang at the top of his voice. His throat quivered, and his breast glowed as red as the holly berries decorating the room. "Oh!" cried the children, and "Oh!" cried the grown-ups, "he's a real one after all, how lovely."

All eyes were on Mr. Robin as he trilled and whistled and chirruped. When at last he stopped, everyone clapped, and the tall man drew back the curtains and opened the window.

"Thank you, little robin," he said, "for making this the best Christmas tree we have ever had. Now fly away home!"

"Goodbye, goodbye, little robin!" called the children, waving to Bob as he flew out into the cold, frosty air. He was so glad to be free that he never once thought of the tinsel.

It was not quite dark, and Bob flew straight to the holly bush. There he found his wife in a terribly anxious state, and so glad to see him that she cared not a bit about the tinsel. They flew back together to the barn, and there she listened open-beaked to the tale of his adventures.

Two or three weeks later when the snow had gone and the sky was blue, and food was plentiful again, Bob found the discarded Christmas tree in the garden.

A few strands of tinsel still hung from it, and when the gardener's back was turned Bob pounced on them eagerly, and took them home to his wife. Mrs. Robin was delighted, and hid them away, and in the spring, when her nest was finished, it was admired by all who saw it.

from The Wise Robin *by Noel Barr*

Remembering the birds

A Scandinavian Christmas Eve tradition is to hang out a sheaf of corn, or other food birds like, fastened to a pole in the garden.

There is much that you can do to help birds through a cold winter. Best of all is a bird-table, placed in the open where you can watch from a window, but preferably near a bush or hedge so that the shyer birds can dart back to cover. If you have no suitable place for a bird-table you can feed them from a window-sill.

Most types of food are suitable to put on or under the bird table: certainly bacon rind or other fat, nuts, fruit, cheese, bread (but not too much white bread), skins from baked potatoes – most leftovers, in fact, as long as they are not too salty or highly seasoned. Fresh water will be much appreciated, especially when everything is frozen. When snow covers the ground, just clearing a patch will help the birds to find insects, spiders and grubs.

Bird mobile

You will need:

 Thin coloured card, glue, sequins, tinsel, coloured tissue paper.

Draw round the template on the coloured card and cut out the shape including the slot. Stick sequins along the top of the bird's head on both sides, using two more sequins for eyes. Cut two short lengths of tinsel to decorate the tail.

Now fold and cut 1 standard sheet of tissue paper into eighths, giving rectangles of 18 x 25cm. Take one small tissue piece and, beginning at the short edge, fold it up concertina-style, ensuring that the width of folds will allow the tissue paper to pass through the slot.

Now snip small triangles from each side of the folded strip.

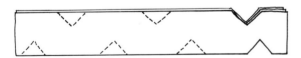

Push the tissue wings through into position, and glue the two inside edges together. When this is dry, unfold the wings and suspend the bird mobile by sewing a long thread through the top of the wings where they join.

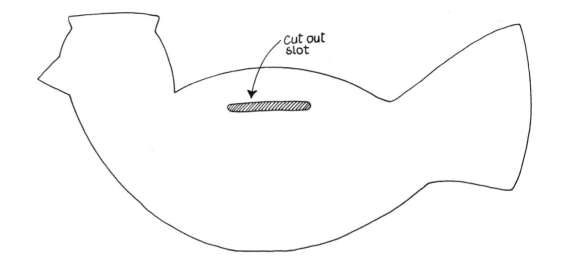

Cut out slot

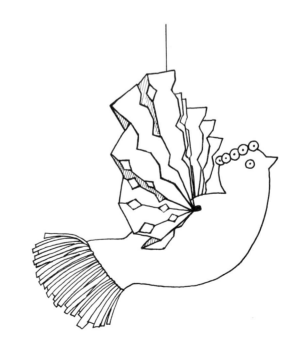

Model animals for the stable scene

These simple animals will blend well with the cylindrical figures on page 40. They are constructed from the same materials and the scale of the animals is appropriate to the height of the figures.

For one animal you will need:
  a cardboard tube from a toilet or paper roll
  a cardboard egg box
  cotton wool, fur fabric, paint, glue

Cut a 'pocket' from the egg box — cut at the base to give the greatest possible circumference.

Insert this into one end of the tube, fixing with glue if necessary. Cut off part of the other end of the tube so that the body is in proportion to the egg box head.

Cut two pieces from two more 'pockets' as shown, to provide two pairs of legs.

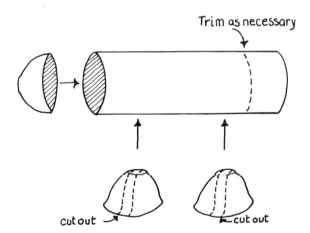

Glue these pairs of legs to the body. Cut ears as required from the flat parts of the box and glue into position.

Cover the body with pieces of fur fabric or cotton wool as appropriate and paint the face and legs.

Why a Donkey was Chosen

One day Reuben was walking down the road. He was thinking about nothing in particular when he saw a notice on a wall. So he went closer, to read it.

Funny notice. It must be in Arabic or Hebrew or upside down!

Wanted:
Elephants, Camels, Horses, Dromedaries, Llamas, Oxen, but not Donkeys.

Not wanted Donkeys. Why not Donkeys?
We Donkeys have lovely ears but they are nothing like an Elephant's ears and we have no trunks or tusks; strange if we had . . .
We Donkeys have lovely eyes but they are nothing like a Camel's eyes and we have no humps; strange if we had . . .
We Donkeys are very strong but not as strong as an Ox and we have no horns like those of an Ox; strange if we had . . .

So Donkeys are not wanted to carry important people, only little people. So I won't apply here will I?

So, while the Elephants, Camels, Horses, Dromedaries, Llamas, Oxen went to apply here, Reuben went to eat some grass.

And while the Elephant was sent to India to carry the Rajah and the Camel was sent to Egypt to carry the Pharaoh and the Horse was sent to Rome to carry the Caesar and the Dromedary, Llama and Ox were sent elsewhere to carry Kings and Sheiks and the Shahs and Queens and the Emperors and Sultans and Tetrachs, Reuben stayed at home and ate grass and waited for someone to carry . . . a little person, perhaps.

And then a man came along and saw Reuben and spoke to him. "I am looking for a beast of burden to carry an important person."
But Reuben shook his head and said: "All the beasts of burden who carry important people have gone far away. I am a Donkey. Donkeys are not wanted to carry important people. We only carry little people. Do you see? . . . Donkeys cannot be too proud."

"I am proud of my ears but they are nothing like an Elephant's ears. I am proud of my eyes but they are nothing like a Camel's eyes. So I have much to be proud of. But not too proud. I have no trunk or tusks or hump or horns. Imagine me if I had!"

The man laughed, and then he said: "This Important Person is also a very little person, for he is an unborn child. He is the Messiah and his name is Jesus. His mother needs to be carried by a beast of burden who cannot be too proud, so I have chosen you, a donkey, to carry her to Bethlehem where her son will be born."

Christopher Gregorowski

Rocking Reindeer

This is a 'stand-up' model of a reindeer that can be used as a place marker at a party or Christmas dinner, a special container for a small present, a decoration to accompany the tree or an ornate Christmas card.

You will need:
- a toilet roll or other cardboard tube
- glue, glitter, sequins, brown paint
- a small stapler
- a piece of thin card 25cm x 11cm (for the reindeer's head)
- a piece of thin coloured card 30cm x 9cm (for the rocker)

On the first piece of card, trace round the template and cut out. Paint the toilet roll brown. Paint the head brown. Spread glue over the antlers and sprinkle with glitter, then turn the double head over and again put glue and glitter onto the antlers. Bend at the nose to give a double-sided head, and staple the two thicknesses of card together just where the antlers and head join. Pull the antlers apart slightly so that all four shiny areas can be seen. Add two sequins for eyes.

Cut pairs of slits into each end of the cardboard tube. They should be 2cm long and must be level since they will house the rocker.

Insert the second piece of card, the rocker, into the pairs of slits and flatten slightly to ensure a good balance.

Now cut two more slits at one end of the tube, near the top, about 1cm apart. The two neck ends of the head will fit into these. Staple the neck ends to the toilet roll to keep them in place.

Some children may want to add further decoration such as a saddle, a figure of Santa Claus or even a sledge for the reindeer to pull. The rocker, too, may be decorated.

The reindeer can be used as a gift-holder, with the wrapped present (if small enough) placed on the rocker. If it is intended as a place-marker or card, the name of the guest, or the greeting, can be written on a strip of white card, stuck on to the inside of the rocker and suitably decorated.

Dee Davidson

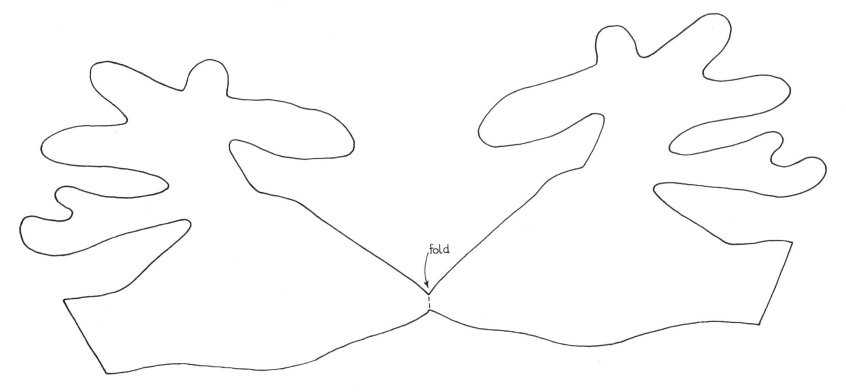

fold

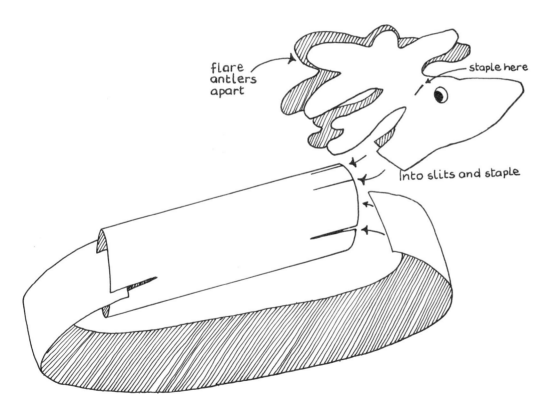

flare antlers apart

staple here

into slits and staple

Reindeer

Reindeer live in arctic or sub-arctic regions of the world; in Canada they are called caribou. Originally they lived wild in large herds and are believed to have existed a million years ago. For centuries they have been domesticated, forming an important factor in the survival of the Eskimos and the Lapps – a source of food, tools (knives were honed from the bones), clothing (from the skins) and transport. One reindeer can carry up to 220 kilograms and can travel for 40 miles a day pulling a loaded sledge.

Reindeer are usually greyish brown with a lighter coloured underside. Both sexes have antlers, although the females' are smaller. The stag drops his antlers in winter whereas the doe keeps hers till spring. Once the old antlers are dropped, new ones appear within two weeks. Male reindeer will fight duels during the rutting season and during this time one stag may gather up to forty females in his 'harem'. Does produce one or two young in each litter. Reindeer feed on grass, birch leaves, willow, lichens, moss and other vegetation.

The traditional idea of reindeer pulling Santa's sledge probably originated from pagan legend. Odin the Norse God galloped across the sky on Sleipnir his white, eight-footed horse, distributing gifts to his people during the feasting that marked the Saturnalia.

Anansi at Christmas

Every year, Mrs Green, our teacher, asks us to help her choose a story for the school's Christmas pantomime for parents. Mrs Green is the music teacher, so she's really in charge of our school plays. Of course, all the other children in our school can be in our pantomime, but usually our class decides which story we will do.

Last year's show was very special for me, because the pantomime we did was really my idea. As usual, Mrs Green asked for ideas. Some people said 'Puss in Boots' and some 'Cinderella'. By the look on her face, I could tell that Mrs Green wasn't really interested in those. I suggested that we could do an Anansi story.

"Well," said Mrs Green. "What a wonderful idea." Then she said: "Perhaps you could tell us all about it."

That's when I wished I'd kept my mouth shut. Mum is always saying that my mouth will get me into trouble one day. Well, that's when it did, because all I knew about Anansi was that the stories came from the West Indies, where my parents came from. I'd read a book about Anansi, and I knew he was a spider who sometimes became a man.

The children all laughed when they heard this, and wanted to hear more. Mrs Green told them that she liked the idea, and would try to find out some more for me.

When I told my dad, he said that he often heard "Nancy" stories, as he knew them, when he was a boy growing up in Guyana, but he didn't remember any.

The next day, Mrs Green told us that she had learnt that Anansi stories came from Africa. She said that the stories were taken to the West Indies by the slaves who remembered them, and told them to their children, who passed them on to their children, and so on.

Mrs Green then wrote some words and songs for us, and chose people from all the classes in school to be in the pantomime. When it was time for us to practise the play, Mrs Green said that we would all have to speak like West Indians, because the play was set in the West Indies. It was really funny hearing English people speaking like West Indians. It wasn't too bad for me because I talked like that at home anyway, but those who didn't had to learn from some of us.

On the night of the play, we all got dressed up and had make-up on – even the boys. I was Anansi the Spiderman, so like a spider I had to have extra legs, and as a man, I had to also wear a straw hat. Other children were made up to look like birds, or pigs, or tortoises, or other animals.

Then, when it was time to begin, the stage lights were switched on and the music started. I got into a hopeless muddle with my legs, and fell over just as I made my first entrance. Everyone laughed because they thought that that was what should happen but not Mrs Green – she just stared at me. Next, David, one of the children from the youngest class, forgot what he had to say. Poor Mrs Green told him in a whisper, which I'm sure everybody heard. We all started laughing even after he was told because David still couldn't say it right.

He managed to get going and at the end all the parents cheered. On the way home, Mum said I was the best Anansi she'd ever seen. Dad said that he remembered hearing the story when he was young, and then began to tell it to me all over again. But by now I was too tired. I fell asleep in the back of the car long before we arrived home.

The Big White Pussy-cat

Once upon a time there was a man. And one day he caught a bear. It was a very fine bear, so he thought he would give it to the King.

So off they went, the man and the bear, tramp, tramp, tramp, to see the King. They hadn't gone very far when they came to a little house. And because it was very dark and they were afraid it was going to snow – because it was winter-time and so cold – they were pleased to see the little house. They knocked at the door to ask if they could come in. They thought, you see, that perhaps they could sleep inside in a cosy bed, instead of outside in the snow. For it would be a long time yet before they got to the King.

A man answered the door. "May we come and sleep in your house?" said the bear-man.

"Oh dear, no," said the man who opened the door. His name was Halvor.

"But it's cold out here," said the bear-man.

"I know," said Halvor.

"So may we come in?" said the bear-man.

"Oh dear, no," said Halvor.

"But it's dark, and it's starting to snow," said the bear-man.

"I know," said Halvor.

"So may we come in?"

"Oh dear, no."

"Well," said the bear-man, "that's a funny way to talk. Don't you want to help us and be kind to us?"

"Oh, I would very much like to help you," said Halvor. "But you see, it's Christmas-time. And every Christmas-time an enormous crowd of trolls come tearing into our house. They bang about, and they break the dishes, and they throw things, and they scream and shout, and they chase us right out of the house! Every Christmas-time! Isn't it a shame for our poor children – they never have a proper Christmas because of those trolls!"

"Oh, is it just trolls that are bothering you?" said the bear-man. "We don't care about trolls. Just let us in and we'll sleep on the floor."

So in the end Halvor let the man and the bear come in. And the bear lay down, while the man sat by the fire. And Halvor and his wife and their three children started to get the Christmas dinner ready; but, do you know, they did it with such sad faces because they knew that the trolls were going to chase them out before they could eat any of it.

Well, the next day was Christmas Day and they put that lovely dinner on the table. And sure enough, down the chimney came the trolls! Through the window came the trolls! Out of the fireplace came the trolls! And they banged about, and they broke the dishes, and they threw things, and they screamed and shouted. Halvor and his wife and the three children got up and ran out of the kitchen and out of the house and into the shed in the garden, and they locked the door. But the man and the bear just sat still and watched. My, oh my, those trolls were naughty. They put their feet on the table, and they put their tails on the table, and they threw milk about, and they squashed up the cakes with their dirty toes, and they licked the jelly with their long, long tongues. The littlest ones were the worst of all. They climbed up the curtains, and they got on the shelves, and they started to throw down all the jars of jam and jars of honey and jars of pickled onions, right off the shelves. Smash! Crash! Oh, there was a mess!

Well, at last one of the littlest naughtiest trolls suddenly saw the bear lying there very quiet and good. And the little troll found a piece of sausage and stuck it on a fork, and waved it about under the bear's nose, and shouted, "Pussy, pussy! Have a sausage!" Oh, he was wild, that little troll! He poked the bear's nose with the fork. And just when the bear snapped at the sausage, he pulled it away so that the bear couldn't get it.

Then the great white bear was very, very angry.

He got up from the floor, and he opened his mouth wide, and he roared at the top of his voice like thunder, and he chased those trolls right out of the house, big ones and little ones, those with tails and those without.

"Good boy!" said the bear-man. "*Good* boy!" And he gave him a whole sausage to eat. And he ate it nicely, making hardly any mess at all.

Then the bear-man called out, "You can come out, Halvor, you and your wife and your three little children. The trolls have gone away. My bear chased them out." So Halvor and his wife and his three children unlocked the wood-shed and came out and came back to the house. They swept up the mess, and they scrubbed the table, and they picked up all the broken bits and put them in the dustbin. Then they all sat down to eat everything the trolls had left – and luckily they had left quite a lot, and it was very nice indeed. Then they all went to bed.

Next day, the bear-man said to Halvor, "Thank you for having us. Now we must go to see the King." And away went the man and the bear, and Halvor never saw them again, so I expect they found the King.

Now when Christmas Eve came round again the next year, Halvor was out chopping wood in the forest. Suddenly he heard someone calling far away through the trees. "Halvor! Halvor!"

"What is it?" shouted Halvor.

"Have you still got your big white pussy-cat with you?"

"Yes, I have!" shouted Halvor. "She's lying in front of the fire at home this minute. And she's got seven kittens now, and each of them is bigger and fiercer than she is herself. Now! What do you say to that?"

"Then, we'll never, never come to see you again!" shouted all the trolls.

And do you know, they never did, never. And now Halvor and his wife and his three children can always eat up their Christmas dinner just the same as everyone else.

Leila Berg

Hugo at Sky Castle

Hugo, a tiny pink larder mouse, has rescued Prince Spring, son of King Summer, from a mousetrap in the larder. The Ogre Winter has locked away King Summer and the Duke of Autumn in the cellar of Sky Castle and thrown the key down to earth. Prince Spring has to find the key, so that he can rescue his father. Having hurt his leg in the mousetrap, he is too unwell to travel, but Hugo bravely volunteers to take the key and go in his place. The Prince summons his friend, Robin Redbreast, who agrees to fly Hugo to Sky Castle, a beautiful yet evil place.

'We're here, look, Sky Castle!'

Hugo squinted into the bright distance, and his first sight of the castle took his breath away.

The two friends pressed on, until the walls towered above them.

Trying to look brave, Hugo gripped the silver key and stepped into the castle, without a backward glance.

Hugo looked around him.

He was standing in a small cobbled courtyard. The castle seemed to lean over staring at him. Hugo made his way across the courtyard to a small door, almost hidden by a yellow mass of winter-flowering jasmine.

Gingerly pushing the door open, he slipped inside, straight into something that made his eyes stand out like chapel hatpegs.

A PAIR OF LONG, WHITE POINTED FEET. 'An icicle!' thought Hugo, holding onto the door, in case its creaking gave him away. Steeling his nerves, the mouse peered upwards. There were two icicles, one standing on either side of the door. Luckily they were looking the other way. They were bigger than the icicles Hugo had seen hanging from the drainpipe at home. They leaned on great swords of sharpened ice. Their uniforms were magnificent: long grey cloaks fell from their shoulders, glistening with magic colours. Brooches

carved from frozen snow shimmered at their necks. Their helmets were of solid ice, tall and graceful, with flowing plumes of winter fog. The plumes and cloaks swirled at the slightest movement. As quietly as only a mouse can, Hugo slid past the terrifying sentinels. He kept in the shadows, hardly daring to breathe. When he was almost clear, his tail brushed the foot of the nearest icicle. Terror stiffened Hugo, his tail stuck out like a poker. The icicle blinked, his eyelashes making a sound like thick ice cracking. To Hugo's relief,

the icicle didn't look down. After a moment, it was safe for the mouse to move, and he slipped past the door and round a bend in the passage. Heartened by his escape, Hugo hurried on, eager to complete his mission and leave this evil place. Rounding a second bend, he came to the head of a flight of stone steps. Unable to stop himself, Hugo plunged off the top step, tumbling head over tail to the blackness below. A frightened squeak forced itself through his long front teeth, as the world turned over. Down and down he fell, unable to save himself, clawing at the spinning staircase.

His cry, and the noise of the tumble, alerted the two icicles. As Hugo bounced to the bottom step, he saw the icicles bounding after him. With their cloaks swirling about them and brandishing their swords, the icicles leapt down the stairs three at a

time. Hugo scrambled to his feet and, not knowing where his courage came from, faced the onslaught.

The leading icicle attacked, his plume streaming behind him, aiming his great sword at Hugo. Hugo danced clear, as the blade missed him by a whisker. He darted between his enemy's legs only to run into the second icicle. The mouse leapt at his new opponent, landing with a thud on the icicle's knees. The guard crashed to the ground, not a pea's length from Hugo. On hitting the ground, the icicle broke into a dozen pieces. But Hugo's joy was short-lived, for as he watched each piece grew into a full-sized, fully armed icicle. For a moment the mouse stood rooted to the spot, his mouth hanging open with surprise. In that moment the army of icicles sprang forward, chattering with rage. They took hold of Hugo, and dragged him away. Hugo was helpless in their chilly grip. What could he do against an enemy who grew stronger at every blow? The icicle ran, hooting and chanting, along dark corridors and through dark chambers. Cobwebs hung everywhere, encrusted in frost, and writhing in the wake of the mad procession.

Poor Hugo, held high by dozens of icy fingers, thought miserably of his mother, and of the world, shivering in the grip of Winter. He was a sad pink larder mouse. He'd failed in his mission.

After what seemed an age, the icicles came to a halt, their way barred by two giant icicles: the Royal Ice Guards!

Although taller than ordinary icicles, their uniforms were the same, except for the helmets. These were made from solid silver, with white plumes, so long that they brushed the ground. In addition to the fearsome swords, the Royal Ice Guards carried slender javelins.

'We have a prisoner to put before the Master,' screeched the icicle, 'Let us pass!' Without a word the Royal Ice Guards stepped aside. They didn't

even glance at Hugo. Hugo was lowered to the floor, and a rough push sent him reeling into the great chamber. The icicles, silent now, hung back. The walls were draped with cobweb silk, dyed in the coldest colours that Hugo had ever seen. Blues, greys and greens, worked into patterns telling stories of the ancient peoples of the skies. The white carpet covering the floor didn't stop the cold biting at Hugo's toes. At the far end of the chamber a short flight of stairs led up to a magnificently carved throne. On the throne, shrouded in shadow, sat the Ogre Winter. Hugo moved a step forward, and looked at him with a mixture of fear and mouselike curiosity.

The Ogre Winter was fat and ugly. His froglike eyes bulged on either side of a long, hooked nose, his skin was coarse, like a doormat. Although he was bald as a bone, Winter had a flowing beard that seemed to change colour as he moved, grey one moment, green the next. In spite of his looking like something out of a rotten apple, Winter wore the most splendid clothes. His shirt and breeches were tailored with great skill.

'Speak now,' growled Winter, 'you'll have precious little chance later!'

from Hugo and the Wicked Winter *by Tony Ross*

Mrs Malone

Mrs Malone
Lived hard by a wood
All on her lonesome
As nobody should.
With her crust on a plate
And her pot on the coal
And none but herself
To converse with, poor soul.
In a shawl and a hood
She got sticks out-o'-door,
On a bit of old sacking
She slept on the floor,
And nobody, nobody
Asked how she fared
Or knew how she managed,
For nobody cared.
    Why make a pother
    About an old crone?
    What for should they bother
    With Mrs Malone?

One Monday in winter
With snow on the ground
So thick that a footstep
Fell without sound,
She heard a faint frostbitten
Peck on the pane
And went to the window
To listen again.
There sat a cock-sparrow
Bedraggled and weak,
With half-open eyelid
And ice on his beak.
She threw up the sash
And she took the bird in,
And mumbled and fumbled it
Under her chin.
    'Ye're all of a smother,
    Ye're fair overblown!
    I've room fer another,'
    Said Mrs Malone.

Come Tuesday while eating
Her dry morning slice
With the sparrow a-picking
('Ain't company nice!')
She heard on her doorpost
A curious scratch,
And there was a cat
With its claw on the latch.
It was hungry and thirsty
And thin as a lath,
It mewed and it mowed
On the slithery path.
She threw the door open
And warmed up some pap,
And huddled and cuddled it
In her old lap.
    'There, there, little brother,
    Ye poor skin-an'-bone,
    There's room fer another,'
    Said Mrs Malone.

Come Wednesday while all of them
Crouched on the mat
With a crumb for the sparrow,
A sip for the cat,
There was wailing and whining
Outside in the wood,
And there sat a vixen
With six of her brood.
She was haggard and ragged
And worn to a shred,
And her half-dozen babies
Were only half fed,
But Mrs Malone, crying
'My! ain't they sweet!'
Happed them and lapped them
And gave them to eat.
    'You warm yerself, mother,
    Ye're cold as a stone!
    There's room fer another,'
    Said Mrs Malone.

Come Thursday a donkey
Stepped in off the road
With sores on his withers
From bearing a load.
Come Friday when icicles
Pierced the white air
Down from the mountainside
Lumbered a bear.
For each she had something,
If little, to give –
'Lord knows, the poor critters
Must all of 'em live.'
She gave them her sacking,
Her hood and her shawl,
Her loaf and her teapot –
She gave them her all.
   'What with one thing and t'other
   Me fambily's grown,
   And there's room fer another,'
   Said Mrs Malone.

Come Saturday evening
When time was to sup
Mrs Malone
Had forgot to sit up.
The cat said *meeow,*
And the sparrow said *peep,*
The vixen, *she's sleeping,*
The bear, *let her sleep.*
On the back of the donkey
They bore her away,
Through trees and up mountains
Beyond night and day,
Till come Sunday morning
They brought her in state
Through the last cloudbank
As far as the Gate.
   'Who is it,' asked Peter,
   'You have with you there?'
   And donkey and sparrow,
   Cat, vixen and bear

Exclaimed, 'Do you tell us
Up here she's unknown?
It's our mother, God bless us!
It's Mrs Malone
Whose havings were few
And whose holding was small
And whose heart was so big
It had room for us all.'
Then Mrs Malone
Of a sudden awoke,
She rubbed her two eyeballs
And anxiously spoke:
'Where am I, to goodness,
And what do I see?
My dears, let's turn back,
This ain't no place fer me!'
   But Peter said, 'Mother
   Go in to the Throne.
   There's room for another
   One, Mrs Malone.'

Eleanor Farjeon

The Legend of the Spider's Web

When Joseph and Mary and Jesus were on their way to Egypt, the story runs, as the evening came they were weary, and they sought refuge in a cave. It was very cold, so cold that the ground was white with hoar frost. A little spider saw the little baby Jesus, and he wished so much that he could do something to keep him warm in the cold night. He decided to do the only thing he could and spin his web across the entrance of the cave, to make, as it were, a curtain there.

Along the path came a detachment of Herod's soldiers, seeking for children to kill to carry out Herod's bloodthirsty order. When they came to the cave they were about to burst in to search it, but their captain noticed the spider's web, covered with the white hoar frost and stretched right across the entrance to the cave. "Look," he said, "at the spider's web there. It is quite unbroken and there cannot possibly be anyone in the cave, for anyone entering would certainly have torn the web."

So the soldiers passed on, and left the holy family in peace, because a little spider had spun his web across the entrance to the cave. And that, so they say, is why to this day we put tinsel on our Christmas trees, for the glittering tinsel streamers stand for the spider's web, white with the hoar frost, stretched across the entrance of the cave on the way to Egypt. It is a lovely story, and this much, at least, is true, that no gift which Jesus receives is ever forgotten.

William Barclay

Farming at Christmas

Farmers are like clergymen and lighthouse keepers in that Christmas is not a time for holidays. Farmers with no livestock may be able to close down, just as a factory shuts down over the Christmas period, but for livestock farmers this is not possible. It is partly a matter of geography: in a southern hemisphere farm Christmas falls in the middle of summer and there are only the routine daily tasks such as (on a dairy farm) milking the cows. But where I live – Scotland – the farm animals depend for their food on the men and women who work with them.

Some animals, such as pigs or hens, may be kept in buildings all the year round and thus require feeding 365 days of the year. In the upland areas of the British Isles, the livestock (principally sheep) will be partly foraging for themselves on the hills, with additional feeding provided when necessary by their shepherds. On the average livestock farm, between four and eight hours a day in winter will be spent feeding and looking after the animals.

Modern machinery has greatly reduced the time it takes to deliver straw, hay and silage (conserved grass) to livestock, whether they are indoors or outdoors. But the number of people working on farms has fallen dramatically over the last thirty years, so although there is less work to do there are fewer people to do it.

Throughout the year the weather is a vital factor for those who work on the farm – and indeed for the animals themselves. Good weather means easier work and working conditions, and more contented animals. So the traditional Christmas card picture with snow lying on the ground is seldom welcomed by the farmer. It can bring all kinds of difficulties: you may have seen pictures on the television of fodder being delivered by helicopter to livestock cut off by snow drifts. For those with animals indoors there may be other difficulties, such as frozen or burst pipes or broken machinery. These problems have to be dealt with immediately as the animals are even less tolerant than human beings of delays at feeding times.

Although the work is not always pleasant at the time, there is a tremendous sense of job satisfaction in farming, both in looking after the animals and in coping with the unexpected problems that arise. At no time are these feelings more pronounced than at Christmas. Having provided so many others with their Christmas dinners gives an added sense of enjoyment when it comes to eating one's own.

David St. Joseph

More songs to sing

Little donkey (*Carol gaily carol 3*)

Hey little bull (*Carol gaily carol 13*)

Jesus our brother, strong and good (*Carol gaily carol 18*)

The cat and the mouse carol (*Merrily to Bethlehem 8*)

All in a wood there grew a tree

Cardboard roll tree

Suitable for wall or board display.

You will need:
 a large cardboard triangle approx 1m high by
  80cm wide at base
 a number of cardboard tubes
 green paint
 glue
 coloured foil scraps

The cardboard tubes should be sliced into 2cm slices; this will be best done beforehand if this activity is to be tackled by very young children.

One circular edge of each ring is spread with, or dipped in, glue. The rings are then stuck all over the triangle, as closely fitting as possible. Young children will enjoy the talking and decision-making involved in placing the rings to achieve the best fit.

When the tree is dry it can be painted green and this becomes a useful exercise in hand control in making the brush cover all the surfaces presented.

When the paint has dried, circles of coloured foil can be stuck inside some rings to decorate, and a 'tub' can be added below.

Smaller models can be made to hang as mobiles, double-sided or with one side painted green.

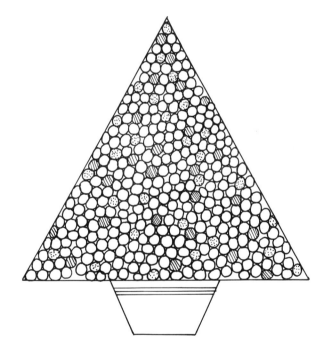

Christmas Tree Biscuits

These are spicy biscuits cut into shapes to hang on the tree. This recipe will give 24 biscuits.

Ingredients:
- 50g soft brown sugar
- 50g margarine or butter
- 5 tbsp. clear honey
- 225g plain flour
- ½ tsp. mixed spice
- ¼ tsp. cinnamon
- ¼ tsp. nutmeg
- ½ tsp. bicarbonate of soda

1. Put the sugar, margarine and honey into a saucepan and heat until the fat has melted. Put aside to cool for a few minutes.
2. Sieve in the flour and spices.
3. Dissolve the bicarbonate in two tsp. of cold water and stir into the mixture.
4. Make the dough into a ball and knead for a minute.
5. Wrap this in clingfilm and chill for about an hour. Set the oven to 375° F, 190° C or gas mark 5.
6. Grease two or three baking trays.
7. Roll out the dough on a floured surface to ½ cm thickness and cut out Christmas shapes, either with cutters or the point of a sharp knife.
8. Arrange the biscuits on the trays, make a hole at the top of each one with a skewer and decorate with chopped nuts, glacé cherries or dried fruit.
9. Bake for 12 to 15 minutes until golden.
10. Transfer the biscuits to a wire cooling rack. When cold, thread lengths of cotton or ribbon through the holes and hang on the tree.

Clay Christmas tree cards

These pretty Christmas cards are best given to the recipient, as they are too fragile to post.

You will need:
- clay (the sort that doesn't need firing)
- poster paints
- varnish
- sequins, beads
- PVA adhesive

Roll out the clay and cut out a tree shape, free-hand or with a biscuit cutter. Use pointed clay tools to etch decorative patterns into the clay. Allow the tree to dry overnight. If your cutter omits the tub, cut out a tub separately and join it to the tree, either while both parts are still wet or by gluing when dry.

Paint the tree, using poster paints. Give it a coat of varnish, and glue on sequins or beads to decorate.

Cut the card to the required size, and fold. Glue the tree onto the card.

An alternative use for these clay trees is as Christmas tree decorations. Make a hole at the top, e.g. using a knitting needle, while the clay is still wet. Paint, varnish and decorate on both sides, and suspend with ribbon or thread. Other shapes can also be made: puddings, stars, bells, snowmen.

Joan Dale

Paper tree

You will need:
  coloured sugar paper (fairly stiff)
  scissors
  ruler
  glue

Cut out a triangle, 40cm high x 25cm wide at the base (or in similar proportion).

Mark branches as shown, using pencil and ruler, leaving a 'trunk' centre panel about 5cm wide. Each branch's thickness can be a ruler's width. Cut along the horizontal lines, taking care not to cut into the trunk.

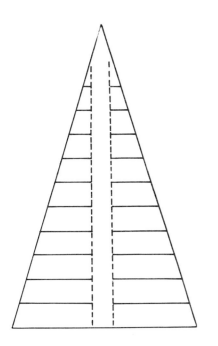

Working from the top (leaving the topmost triangle) take the first pair of branches and glue or staple them together in front to form a ring. Leave the next pair free, then staple every alternate pair of branches.

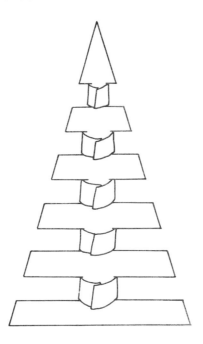

Stick onto card or paper of a contrasting colour, to use as a picture. Several trees treated thus make a most effective background for a classroom frieze. Miniature versions can be stuck onto coloured card and used for calendars.

Tree mobile

A variation of this idea is to make a pair of trees and stick them back-to-back by gluing along one of the trunks. (Do this *before* the branch rings have been joined up.) Make a loop of thread at the top and suspend.

Lynda Martyn

Christmas Tree

In the dark,
And in the snow,
Up and down
The street I go.

In every window
I can see
A shimmering,
Shining Christmas tree.

They look so pretty,
Look so fine,
I skip right home
To look at mine.

B. J. Lee

Christmas is in the air

Christmas is in the air
Everywhere.
And I simply have to stop
At the village shop
And stare.
For where there used to be
Eggs and butter, cheese and tea
Now in splendour there I see
A Christmas tree.

Alison Winn

Christmas tree, straight and tall

Christmas tree, straight and tall,
Shedding light upon us all.
Decorations shiny and new,
How we love to look at you.
   Lovely things hung all around,
   With your fairy high above the ground,
Christmas tree, new and green,
Finest tree we've ever seen.

Stuart Johnson

3-part ostinato for chime bars

notes used:

Silver snowflakes for the Christmas tree

For each snowflake you will need:
   3½ pipe cleaners (i.e. the 4th to be cut in half)
   narrow strips of foil, approx 1½–2 cm wide
   a length of tinsel (approx 20 cm)

These attractive star-like snowflakes provide an almost instant tree decoration or mobile. They are quickly made, and require no glue or tape to hold them together.

Bind each of the three full-length pipecleaners with the strips of foil, wrapping around and pinching to keep in position. Place the three foil-clad sticks in a six-pointed star shape, and use the remaining (uncovered) half-stick to fix the shape, winding it round where the three sticks cross at the centre. Then wind the tinsel round to conceal the join and form a glittering central ball.

Hang the snowflakes from the Christmas tree, where they will catch the light beautifully, or suspend them by thread to form a mobile. Larger ones can be made by using extra-large pipecleaners (available from school suppliers) or by joining short ones together (overlapping and twisting together).

The Christmas Tree

The custom of decorating a tree for Christmas came from Germany where, in the medieval mystery plays, a fir tree represented the Garden of Eden and was hung with apples and ringed with candles.

One legend suggests that Martin Luther, the great reformer, was walking through a star-lit forest one night and was so moved by the sight of the stars shining through the fir trees' branches that, on returning home, he related this to his children comparing it to a vision of Jesus bringing light from heaven to earth. This notion may well have inspired people to bring trees indoors and to decorate them with candles.

In the 19th century Prince Albert, Queen Victoria's consort, popularized the Christmas tree when he installed one at Windsor. The decorations on this Victorian tree included nuts and sweets in baskets, oranges, stars, dolls, lanterns and candles.

The fairy or angel that we are accustomed to seeing on the topmost branch was originally a figure of the infant Jesus.

The huge fir tree that stands in London's Trafalgar Square is sent annually by the Norwegians to thank Britain for her help during the Second World War. The tree is shipped from Oslo and arrives about a month before Christmas. It is erected and decorated with white lights in the traditional Norwegian fashion. The lighting up ceremony takes place during the second week of December when the Norwegian ambassador switches on the lights accompanied by the Lord Mayor of Westminster. The tree is lit thereafter every day from 3pm until midnight throughout the Christmas period, finishing on Twelfth Night. Carol singers gather to sing each evening until Christmas Eve.

In the United States, the President switches on the lights that decorate the tree that stands on the White House lawn.

Christmas with the Victorian Royal Family

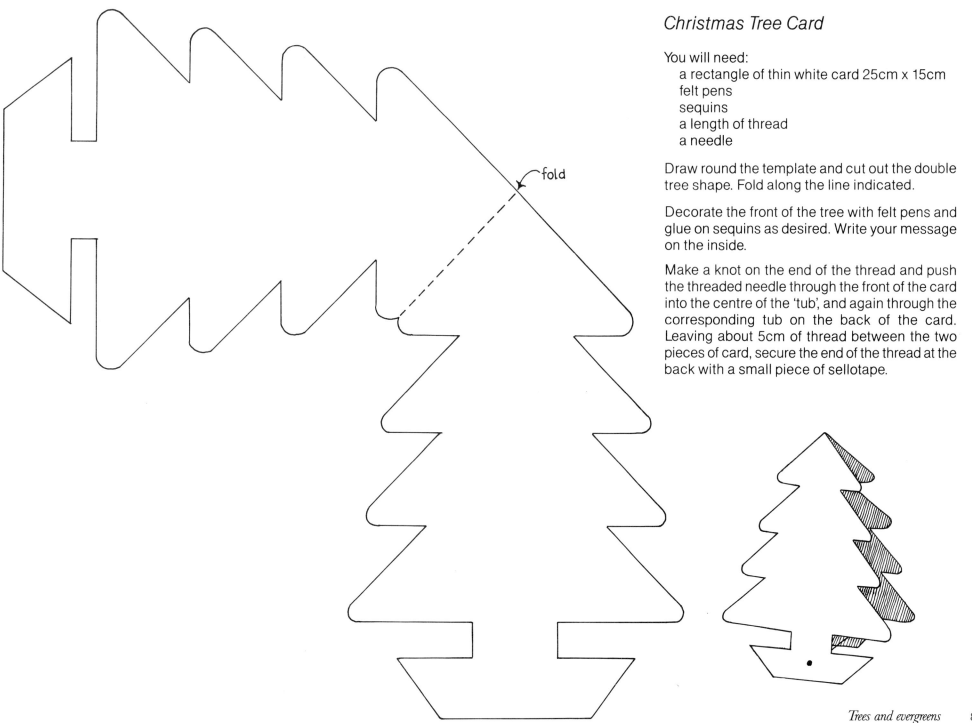

Christmas Tree Card

You will need:
- a rectangle of thin white card 25cm x 15cm
- felt pens
- sequins
- a length of thread
- a needle

Draw round the template and cut out the double tree shape. Fold along the line indicated.

Decorate the front of the tree with felt pens and glue on sequins as desired. Write your message on the inside.

Make a knot on the end of the thread and push the threaded needle through the front of the card into the centre of the 'tub', and again through the corresponding tub on the back of the card. Leaving about 5cm of thread between the two pieces of card, secure the end of the thread at the back with a small piece of sellotape.

fold

Mistletoe

Mistletoe was known as the 'golden bough', for if stored indoors for a year it became slightly gilded. In ancient times it was distributed by the Druids when they gathered for the Winter Solstice celebrations on December 21st, the shortest day of the year. These mystics considered this plant to be so sacred that they would cut it only with a golden blade.

Mistletoe is ascribed many properties, such as the power to keep storms at bay, but nowadays it is used most commonly in the 'Kissing-bough' suspended in halls and doorways. Under the mistletoe any boy may demand a kiss from a girl, who should complete the tradition by plucking a berry and throwing it over her shoulder.

Mistletoe kissing bough

You will need:
  2 wire hoops
  sellotape
  tinsel
  lametta (thin foil strands)
  foil
  a card egg box
  green crêpe paper
  holly
  ivy
  mistletoe

Cover the hoops by winding crêpe paper strips around them. Fix them together at right-angles with sellotape or string.

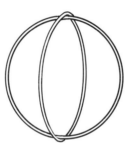

Stick holly sprigs or wind ivy on top of the crêpe paper all around the loops. Cut three 'pockets' from the egg box and cover with foil to make bells. Suspend these on different lengths of thread to hang inside the loops. Hang the bunch of mistletoe below and decorate the kissing bough with lengths of tinsel or lametta strands. Position yourself under the hanging bough and wait for some Christmas kisses!

If the kissing-bough is intended as a large hanging feature in a school hall or foyer, plastic P.E. hoops could be used instead to make a larger and more dramatic display.

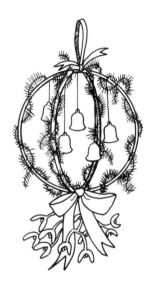

The Christmas tree, and its relations

The tree which finds its way into millions of homes as 'Christmas tree' is the *Norway Spruce*, which originally came from the mountains of Scandinavia and North-West Russia but is now grown widely in Britain and many other countries as a source of timber for building and also paper-making.

Spruces form one family of conifers (cone-bearing trees). There are many others, mostly evergreen, and a tree identification book will help the observer distinguish between spruce, pine, fir, cedar or cypress. One common conifer, the larch, is deciduous, shedding its needle-leaves in autumn along with most of the broad-leafed trees.

In wintertime the Christmas evergreens – holly, ivy and mistletoe—can readily be spotted in woodland or garden or by the roadside, and there are also other evergreens to watch out for: yew, bay, box and privet.

The Yule Log

The word *Yule* is probably derived from the Anglo-Saxon name *Ialkr* (pronounced 'yeolka') meaning Odin, the Norse God. The people of Northern Europe held a mid-winter feast in his honour to celebrate the sun's rebirth. Odin was supposed to have galloped across the sky distributing gifts to all.

The large logs that were burned during the feast not only gave warmth and light to people during the intensely cold, dark winter, but were also thought to help in summoning the sun to return to the sky.

The Yule log then became an established tradition with many attendant customs. Once the log had been selected it was bedecked with ribbons and ceremoniously dragged home by lines of jubilant revellers. A man who purchased his log was considered unlucky, the implication being that he would be too idle and selfish to work sufficiently hard during the next harvest season.

While the Yule log burned, ash was removed and mixed with corn-seed which provided a lucky charm against evil. The charred fragments were retained during the forthcoming year to ward off wicked spirits, and then used finally to kindle the next year's Yule log.

Holly, Ivy – Evergreens

The custom of decorating homes with wreaths and sprays of greenery began when our pagan ancestors, forced to endure hard, cold winters, took great comfort from the evergreen leaves of holly, laurel and ivy etc. finding them a sign of luck and a promise of spring to come.

Give me holly, bold and jolly

Give me holly, bold and jolly,
Honest, prickly, shining holly;
Pluck me holly leaf and berry
For the day when I make merry.

Christina Rossetti

Riddle

Highty tighty, paradighty,
Clothed all in green,
The King could not read it,
No more could the queen;
They sent for the wise men
From out of the East,
Who said it had horns,
But was not a beast.

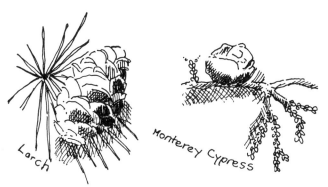

Larch

Monterey Cypress

Cedar of Lebanon

Scots Pine

Song suggestions

Now the holly bears a berry (the Sans Day Carol) (*Merrily to Bethlehem* 32)

O Christmas Tree (*Carol gaily carol* 41)

My true love gave to me

Gifts and giving

The New Baby King

Once upon a time there lived a woman called Mary. Mary was sweeping up the floor when an angel came along. "You are going to get a baby boy, and you must call him Jesus." Mary was so happy that she went to see her husband called Joseph. But Joseph said, "We are going to Bethlehem to pay our taxes."

Mary went on a donkey. The day went slowly. At night they arrived.

Joseph asked the first innkeeper. "No", he said. The second innkeeper said "No". The third innkeeper said, "I haven't got any rooms, but we have got a stable." "May I see?" said Joseph.

At night baby Jesus was born. Mary wrapped him with her blanket.

The shepherds were walking along when they saw an angel. "You must follow that shining star and it will lead you to Bethlehem where the new baby king is born." "Oh what shall we take for the king?" "Why don't we take a baby lamb," said a shepherd.

The kings were out to take presents to the new baby king. The presents were gold, myrrh and frankincense.

Soon they arrived at the stable. "I will give the baby gold," said the first king. "I will give the baby frankincense," said the second king. "I will give the baby myrrh," said the third king.

The shepherds arrived at the stable. "I will give presents to the baby king."

Mary said "Thank you for all your loving presents".

"Thank you," she said.

Michelle Parekh, 8
and Chalene Chandrasiri, 8

Morris's Disappearing Bag

It was Christmas morning. "Wow!" said Morris.

Morris's brother, Victor, got a hockey outfit.

Morris's sister, Rose, got a beauty kit.

Morris's other sister, Betty, got a chemistry set.

And Morris got a bear.

All Christmas Day Victor played hockey and Rose made herself beautiful and Betty mixed acids.

And then Betty made herself beautiful and Victor sorted test tubes and Rose played left wing.

And then Victor made himself beautiful and Betty played goalie and Rose invented a new gas.

Morris was too young to play with chemicals, said Betty, he might blow up the house.

He was too little to play hockey, said Victor, he might get hurt.

And he was too silly to use the beauty kit, said Rose, he would waste all the lipstick.

Nobody wanted Morris's bear.

"Come", said Morris's mother, "let's make a hat for your bear."

"No!" said Morris.

"Let's take your bear for walk," suggested Morris's father.

"No!" said Morris.

Morris wouldn't eat his dinner. "What's the matter with Morris?" asked his father. "I think he hit himself with the hockey puck," said Victor. "Maybe he ate the lipstick," said Rose. "It was the gas," said Betty, "He breathed it in."

Morris sat under the Christmas tree. Suddenly he noticed a package that had been overlooked.

He opened it. In it was a Disappearing Bag.

Morris crawled right in.

"Morris?" said Victor.

"Right here," said Morris.

"Where?" asked Victor.

"Where's Morris?" asked Betty and Rose.

"Over here," said Morris.

But they couldn't find him.

"Maybe he blew himself up," said Betty. "Do you suppose he's so beautiful we wouldn't recognize him?" asked Rose. "Dad!" shouted Victor, "Morris is skating so fast we can't see him."

Morris came out of his bag.

"Where were you?" asked Victor. "I was in my Disappearing Bag," said Morris. "I want to use it," shouted Victor. "Me first," said Rose. "You can use my chemicals," said Betty.

Morris held open his bag. Everybody disappeared at once.

Then he zoomed, and mixed, and beautified, until bedtime.

"Bedtime!" said Morris.

"May I use the bag tomorrow?" asked Rose.

"I want to sleep in it tonight," said Betty.

"Morris," said Victor, "I hope you remember where you put the bag."

But Morris was already fast asleep.

Rosemary Wells

Pass the parcel

Pass the parcel, pass it all along.
Careful not to drop it on the floor!
Pass the parcel till the end of the song,
Then pass it   *   times more.

When you get to   *   choose a different number each time. (Perhaps get someone who can't see the action to choose it.) When you've sung the song, everybody counts while the parcel is passed on the chosen number of times.

Pass   the par - cel,   pass   it   all   a - long.

Care - ful   not   to   drop   it   on   the   floor!

Pass   the par - cel   till   the   end   of   the   song,   then

pass   it   *   times   more.

Jan Holdstock

Chocolate and coconut shortbread

These biscuits have a delicious 'nutty' flavour, are not over-sweet and have proved enormously popular with children and adults alike. They can easily be made at school and will make a welcome gift.

Preheat oven to 350°F, 200°C, gas mark 4

Ingredients:
    200g margarine
    100g dark brown sugar
    100g dessicated coconut
    150g plain wholemeal flour
    50g cocoa powder (or carob flour)

1. Melt the margarine in a saucepan over a low heat.
2. Remove the pan from the heat and add the sugar, stirring well.
3. Add all the other ingredients and mix well.
4. Spoon the mixture into two round 7-inch tins and press down firmly with a fork. (Do not grease the tins.) Bake for 20-25 mins, checking after 20 mins as the edges are inclined to burn.
5. Remove from the oven. Leave for a few minutes, then cut into 8 pieces per tin. Leave to cool in the tin, then lift out carefully. It will keep well in an air-tight container.
6. If larger quantities are required, use a baking-tin and cut the shortbread into squares.

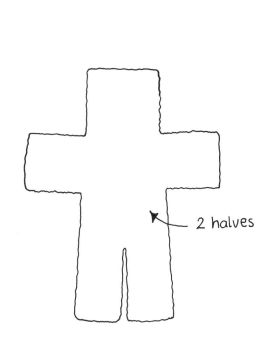

2 halves

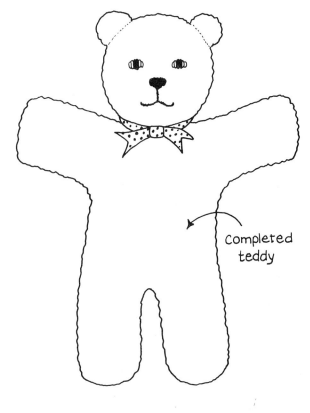

Completed teddy

Knitted Teddy

This teddy pattern is extremely simple and ideal for beginners to learn on. It is knitted throughout in garter stitch (plain knitting). One class of seven and eight year olds completed theirs within a term and thereafter pestered their teacher for patterns of clothes that they might knit, so that the teddies were finally displayed in jumpers, skirts, shorts, capes, shoes and handbags! They make admirable gifts for younger brothers and sisters.

You will need: 2oz double knitting wool, no. 9 needles.

Make two pieces alike:
Cast on 10 stitches. Knit 36 rows. Leave stitches on a safety pin. Repeat this. Knit across both sets of stitches for 24 rows.

Cast on 14 stitches at the beginning of the next two rows. Knit 16 rows.

Cast off 14 stitches at the beginning of the next two rows.

Knit 30 rows on the remaining 20 stitches. Cast off.

Join the two halves by oversewing round the edges, leaving the top of the head open. Turn inside out. Stuff lightly with washable stuffing. Oversew along the top of the head. Stitch through the head-corners for ears. Embroider the features and tie a ribbon round its neck.

A Busy Day

William awoke and rubbed his eyes. It was Christmas Day – the day to which he had looked forward with mingled feelings for twelve months. It was a jolly day, of course – presents and turkey and crackers and staying up late. On the other hand, there were generally too many relations about, too much was often expected of one, the curious taste displayed by people who gave one presents often marred one's pleasure.

He looked round his bedroom expectantly. On the wall, just opposite his bed, was a large illuminated card hanging by a string from a nail – "A Busy Day is a Happy Day." That had not been there the day before. Brightly-coloured roses and forget-me-nots and honeysuckle twined round all the words. William hastily thought over the three aunts staying in the house, and put it down to Aunt Lucy. He looked at it with a doubtful frown. He distrusted the sentiment.

A copy of "Portraits of our Kings and Queens" he put aside as beneath contempt. "Things a Boy Can Do" was more promising. *Much* more promising. After inspecting a penknife, a pocket-compass, and a pencil-box (which shared the fate of "Portraits of our Kings and Queens"), William returned to "Things a Boy Can Do." As he turned the pages, his face lit up.

He leapt lightly out of bed and dressed. Then he began to arrange his own gifts to his family. For his father he had bought a bottle of highly-coloured sweets, for his elder brother Robert (aged nineteen) he had expended a vast sum of money on a copy of "The Pirates of the Bloody Hand." These gifts had cost him much thought. The knowledge that his father never touched sweets, and that Robert professed scorn of pirate stories, had led him to hope that the recipients of his gifts would make no objection to the unobtrusive theft of them by their recent donor in the course of the next few days. For his grown-up sister Ethel he had bought a box of coloured chalks. That also might come in useful later. Funds now had been running low, but for his mother he had bought a small cream jug which, after fierce bargaining, the man had let him have at half-price because it was cracked.

Singing "Christians Awake!" at the top of his lusty young voice, he went along the landing, putting his gifts outside the doors of his family, and pausing to yell "Happy Christmas" as he did so. From within he was greeted in each case by muffled groans.

He went downstairs into the hall, still singing. It was earlier than he thought – just five o'clock.

from More William *by Richmal Crompton*

Shops at Christmas

O the pickled onions looking through the
    jars,
Just waiting for someone to buy them!

The clothes in the shops, all decorated and
    looking gay,
And all the nice, funny people!

The sweets in the windows,
Just waiting to be eaten!

O, come on, Christmas!

Janis Baker, 10

Angels in hoods and mittens

Another bang of the street door sent the basket under the sofa, and the girls to the table, eager for breakfast.

"Merry Christmas, Marmee! Many of them! Thank you for our books; we read some, and mean to every day," they cried in chorus.

"Merry Christmas, little daughters! I'm glad you began at once, and hope you will keep on. But I want to say one word before we sit down. Not far away from here lies a poor woman with a little new-born baby. Six children are huddled into one bed to keep from freezing, for they have no fire. There is nothing to eat over there; and the oldest boy came to tell me they were suffering hunger and cold. My girls, will you give them your breakfast as a Christmas present?"

They were all unusually hungry, having waited nearly an hour, and for a minute no one spoke; only a minute, for Jo exclaimed impetuously –

"I'm so glad you came before we began!"

"May I go and help carry the things to the poor little children!" asked Beth eagerly.

"I shall take the cream and the muffins," added Amy, heroically giving up the articles she most liked.

Meg was already covering the buckwheats, and piling the bread into one big plate.

"I thought you'd do it," said Mrs. March, smiling as if satisfied. "You shall all go and help me, and when we come back we will have bread and milk for breakfast, and make it up at dinner-time."

They were soon ready, and the procession set out. Fortunately it was early, and they went through back streets, so few people saw them, and no one laughed at the queer party.

A poor, bare, miserable room it was, with broken windows, no fire, ragged bedclothes, a sick mother, wailing baby, and a group of pale, hungry children cuddled under one old quilt, trying to keep warm.

How the big eyes stared and the blue lips smiled as the girls went in!

'Ach, mein Gott! it is good angels come to us!' said the poor woman, crying for joy.

"Funny angels in hoods and mittens," said Jo, and set them laughing.

In a few minutes it really did seem as if kind spirits had been at work there. Hannah, who had carried wood, made a fire, and stopped up the broken panes with old hats and her own cloak. Mrs. March gave the mother tea and gruel, and comforted her with promises of help, while she dressed the little baby as tenderly as if it had been her own. The girls, meantime, spread the table, set the children round the fire, and fed them like so many hungry birds – laughing, talking, and trying to understand the funny broken English.

"Das is gut!" "Die Engelkinder!" cried the poor things, as they ate, and warmed their purple hands at the comfortable blaze.

The girls had never been called angel children before, and thought it very agreeable. That was a very happy breakfast, though they didn't get any of it; and when they went away, leaving comfort behind, I think there were not in all the city four merrier people than the hungry little girls who gave away their breakfasts and contented themselves with bread and milk on Christmas morning.

from Little Women *by Louisa M. Alcott*

Paper plate calendars

A paper plate is an ideal basis for a calendar and can be decorated in many ways. Some ideas are listed below, but the variations are endless. The raised plate rim should be left plain since it provides a frame for the art-work in the centre.

(a) Cut-out pictures from Christmas cards or magazines
(b) Felt-tip pen drawings
(c) Glue 'trailed' and then sprinkled with glitter
(d) Different pasta shapes stuck on and sprayed with metallic paint
(e) A face (clown, Santa etc) painted on
(f) Fabric collage
(g) Sewn patterns using wool or coloured embroidery thread (with holes 'stabbed' by the teacher beforehand if necessary)

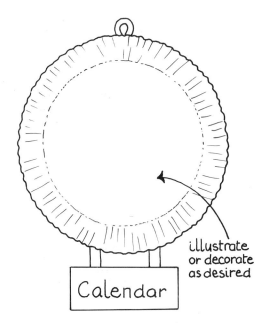

illustrate or decorate as desired

Calendar

Christmas cards

The first Christmas card is believed to have been sent by Henry Cole in 1843. He asked his friend, the artist John Horsley, to design a card, and a thousand copies were made, each one selling for one shilling – a huge sum at that time.

The idea of coloured Christmas greetings only became popular when new printing processes were developed, making the cards much cheaper.

The first post office rush came in 1870 with the sale of a special half-penny stamp, and in 1880 the Postmaster General first used the now famous phrase, "Post early for Christmas!"

Ideas for Christmas cards

1 Get pieces of card or paper. Fold them in half and then stick your old pictures on the front.

2 Cut out stars and bell shapes in gold or silver paper and stick them on the front of your cards. You can decorate a bell shape by sticking a bow of ribbon on top. The clapper can be made by threading a bead on to some cotton and threading it through the card so that it hangs down.

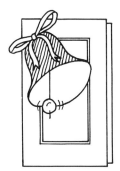

3 Holly leaves can be cut out of green paper and berries can be added by sticking or sewing red beads to the card.

4 The Father Christmas and Christmas pudding are easy to draw as they are mostly circles. Father Christmas could have a red nose to match his hat — and why not stick a few real currants on the Christmas pudding?

 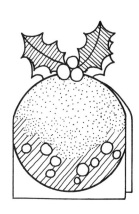

When making gifts, cards or decorations, bear in mind that educational suppliers include in their catalogues numerous items of particular use at Christmas, e.g. card blanks, unwaxed paper plates, gold and silver pens, frankincense and myrrh, 3-D pulp shapes, doilies . . .

A Pop-up card

You will need: ruler, scissors, crayons, glue, stiff paper.

1 Cut two pieces of paper about 20cm x 30cm. Fold them in half then open them out flat.

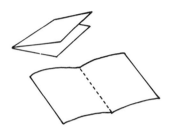

2 Inside one piece, draw a square in the middle about 10cm x 10cm.

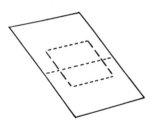

3 Draw a picture on it with the part you want to pop up inside the square.

4 Cut along the two sides of the square.

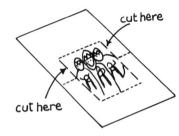

cut here

cut here

5 Cut round the top of your pop-up but do not cut the 'shoulders' at the sides.

cut here

do not cut here

6 Crease and fold forwards along the top and bottom of the square (along the dotted lines).

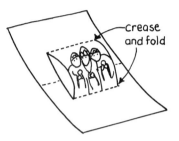

crease and fold

7 Crease the shoulders and fold.

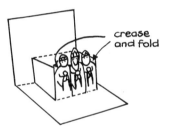

crease and fold

8 Use glue at the edges to stick the pop-up inside the second piece of folded paper.

glue round edge

Sewn Christmas card

This is a suitable activity for fairly inexperienced sewers of 7 or 8 years.

You will need:
    piece of card approx 22cm x 36cm
    rectangle of closely woven white (or pale-
       coloured) plain fabric approx 16cm x 20cm
    pencil
    needle and green embroidery thread
    scraps of coloured felt
    some sequins
    glue

Using pencil, draw a *simple* Christmas tree outline on the fabric, leaving at least 2cm border along the top and sides and 4cm along the bottom (to allow for later addition of a tub).

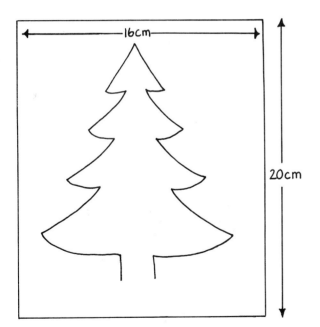

Using needle and green thread, do running stitches along the pencil outline.

Using a fresh length of thread and keeping the needle on the upper side of the fabric, join up the running stitches by slipping the needle under each stitch in turn, giving the effect of a solid unbroken line.

Iron the fabric to flatten any puckering. Fold the card in half and stick the fabric on to the front. Cut a tub from the felt scraps and stick in position. For decoration stick on sequins or small felt pieces cut to represent parcels, candles or baubles. Wool strands, particularly textured yarns such as bouclé or mohair, make effective streamers.

The Computer's first Christmas card

```
jollymerry
hollyberry
jollyberry
merryholly
happyjolly
jollyjelly
jellybelly
bellymerry
hollyheppy
jollyMolly
marryJerry
merryHarry
hoppyBarry
heppyJarry
boppyheppy
berryjorry
jorryjolly
moppyjelly
Mollymerry
Jerryjolly
bellyboppy
jorryhoppy
hollymoppy
Barrymerry
Jarryhappy
happyboppy
boppyjolly
jollymerry
merrymerry
merrymerry
merryChris
ammerryasa
Chrismerry
asMERRYCHR
YSANTHEMUM
```

Edwin Morgan

Heart baskets

You will need:
  two rectangles of paper (different colours), each 9cm x 24cm.

Fold each piece of paper in half lengthways and round off the open corners with scissors.

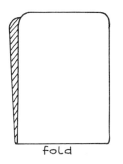 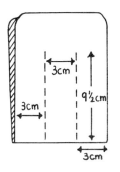

Draw two lines on each folded piece as shown, 9½cm long, giving three prongs of 3cm width. Cut along these lines.

Weave the prongs together as shown.

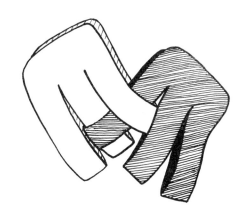

Add a paper strip handle and fill the basket with small sweets before hanging on the tree.

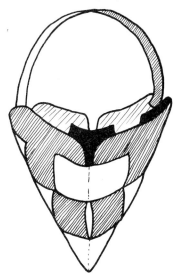

The Elves and the Shoemaker

There was once a shoemaker who worked very hard and was very honest; but still he could not earn enough to live upon, and at last all he had in the world was gone, except just leather enough to make one pair of shoes. Then he cut them all ready to make up the next day, meaning to get up early in the morning to work. His conscience was clear and his heart light amidst all his troubles; so he went peaceably to bed, left all his cares to heaven, and fell asleep. In the morning, after he had said his prayers, he set himself down to his work, when, to his great wonder, there stood the shoes, all ready made, upon the table. The good man knew not what to say or think of this strange event. He looked at the workmanship; there was not one false stitch in the whole job; and all was so neat and true, that it was a complete masterpiece.

That same day a customer came in, and the shoes pleased him so well that he willingly paid a price higher than usual for them; and the poor shoemaker with the money bought leather enough to make two pairs more. In the evening he cut out the work, and went to bed early that he might get up and begin betimes next day: but he was saved all the trouble, for when he got up in the morning the work was finished ready to his hand. Presently in came buyers, who paid him handsomely for his goods, so that he bought leather enough for four pairs more. He cut out the work again over night, and found it finished in the morning as before; and so it went on for some time: what was got ready in the evening was always done by daybreak, and the good man soon became thriving and prosperous again.

One evening about Christmas time, as he and his wife were sitting over the fire chatting together, he said to her, 'I should like to sit up and watch tonight, that we may see who it is that comes and does my work for me.' The wife liked the thought; so they left a light burning, and hid themselves in the corner of the room behind a curtain that was hung up there, and watched what should happen.

As soon as it was midnight, there came two little naked dwarfs; and they sat themselves upon the shoemaker's bench, took up all the work that was cut out, and began to ply with their little fingers, stitching and rapping and tapping away at such a rate, that the shoemaker was all amazement, and could not take his eyes off for a moment. And on they went till the job was quite finished, and the shoes stood ready for use upon the table. This was long before daybreak; and then they bustled away as quick as lightning.

The next day the wife said to the shoemaker, 'These little wights have made us rich, and we ought to be thankful to them, and do them a good office in return. I am quite vexed to see them run about as they do; they have nothing upon their backs to keep off the cold. I'll tell you what, I will make each of them a shirt, and a coat and waistcoat, and a pair of pantaloons into the bargain; do you make each of them a little pair of shoes.'

The thought pleased the good shoemaker very much; and one evening, when all the things were ready, they laid them on the table instead of the work that they used to cut out, and then went and hid themselves to watch what the little elves would do. About midnight they came in, and were going to sit down to their work as usual; but when they saw the clothes lying for them, they laughed and were greatly delighted. Then they dressed themselves in the twinkling of an eye, and danced and capered and sprang about as merry as could be, till at last they danced out at the door over the green; and the shoemaker saw them no more: but every thing went well with him from that time forward, as long as he lived.

from Grimms' Fairy Tales

Uncooked sweets as gifts – peppermint fondant creams and chocolate truffles

Both kinds of confectionery can be made in the classroom and without a cooker. They make acceptable gifts, especially when presented attractively. Either arrange them in petit-four cases set out on a painted or covered circular cheese-box and sealed with clingfilm, or wrap the sweets individually in squares of clingfilm and fill home-made boxes or paper cups, suitably decorated.

Peppermint fondant creams

Ingredients:
  2 egg whites
  1lb icing sugar
  few drops peppermint essence

1. Whisk the egg whites till frothy.
2. Gradually whisk in the sugar until the fondant is too stiff to whisk and then use a wooden spoon for mixing in the remaining sugar.
3. Mix in the essence.
4. Roll out the fondant on a surface dusted with icing sugar.
5. Cut out shapes with cutters. Leave the creams to set firmly before packaging.

Chocolate truffles

Ingredients:
  2oz cake crumbs
  2oz grated chocolate
  1 tbs chocolate powder or cocoa
  grated rind of an orange
  1 tsp apricot jam
  chocolate vermicelli (to coat)

1. Mix all the ingredients together – except the vermicelli.
2. Take teaspoonfuls and roll into small balls about 3cm in diameter. Roll these in the vermicelli.
3. Keep in an airtight container or tin until you are ready to package them as gifts.

Horace's Christmas Disappointment

Young Horace Giraffe on Christmas Eve
Put out his stocking to receive
Whatever Santa Claus might bring.
You may indeed be wondering
What sort of size such stockings are,
Since even small giraffes are far
Bigger than quite a tall man is.
Young Horace Giraffe had measured his,
And found it stretched four feet or so
From ample top to roomy toe.

What piles and piles of presents he
Imagined packed there presently!
A hundred tangerines; a bunch
Of ripe bananas for his lunch;
Five watermelons; fifty figs;
The most delicious juicy sprigs
Plucked from the tops of special trees
With leaves as sweet as honey-bees;
And in the very bottom, some
Chocolates full of candied rum.

Alas, poor Horace! Christmas Day
Dawned, and he rose from where he lay
To snatch the stocking from the bed –
But though it bulged, he felt with dread
How light it was . . . He reached inside –
And then he very nearly died.

Inside the stocking, almost half
The size of Horace, was a SCARF
(A useful garment, yes, I know,
But oh, it was a bitter blow.)
The scarf was fully ten yards long,
And striped and bright and very strong.
It filled the stocking, top to toe,
And Horace was quite filled with woe.

The moral is: A *USEFUL* PRESENT
  IN STOCKINGS IS RATHER
  SELDOM PLEASANT.

Anthony Thwaite

A Gift for Gramps

'What are you going to give Gramps for Christmas?' Louella asked her brother as she stared at her Christmas list.

'That's just what I was going to ask you,' replied Johnny. 'I'm stumped.' The two children were sitting alone at the kitchen table. Their half-finished Christmas lists lay before them.

'Gramps always gets socks and handkerchiefs – handkerchiefs and socks,' continued Johnny. 'He has enough to last another hundred years!'

'I know,' said Louella. 'And we can't get him sports things because with his legs 'so full of rheumatism, poor Gramps just sits in his chair by the window. I wish we could think of something that would be fun for him every day to help him forget his pain.'

So they thought and they thought. Louella closed her eyes, and Johnny stared out of the window at the snowy yard. As he watched, a quick little bird flew to the window-sill, looked into the room, and then flew away.

Suddenly Johnny jumped up from his chair in great excitement. 'I've got it!' he shouted.

'Got what?' asked Louella.

'Why, the present for Gramps. It's perfect, and the whole family could be in on it!'

On Christmas morning, when Gramps had hobbled to his favourite chair by the window, Johnny said, 'Gramps, we wanted to give you something different this year. Something that would be fun for a long time. Now turn around, and look out of the window!'

Gramps turned to look. There, attached to the sill, was a wide new shelf with a moulding around its edge. And on the shelf were all sorts of things that birds like to eat: seeds and suet and dabs of peanut butter and bits of dry bread.

'I made the feeding-station,' Johnny explained. 'And Louella got the supply of bird food for you,

Gramps.' Johnny held his breath as he saw a snowbird perch on the edge of the feeding-station and then fearlessly peck at some seeds.

'Well, I'll be . . .' Gramps said. 'Look at that!'

Then, with a red and grey flash of wings, another bird swooped down.

'What in the world kind of bird is that?' asked Gramps.

'Ah,' said mother, 'that's where my present comes in.' She reached under the boughs of the Christmas tree and pulled out a package which was hidden there. 'Merry Christmas, Grandpa!'

Gramps opened the package excitedly. There before him was a big book with beautiful coloured pictures of hundreds of birds.

'Well, this is something!' Gramps exclaimed, turning the pages. 'I never knew there were so many birds.'

Sometime later, Gramps gave a shout. 'A pine grosbeak! That's what that red and grey bird was: a pine grosbeak!' He grinned with pleasure at being such a good detective. He had forgotten all about his aching rheumatism!

'This is the best Christmas present I ever got,' Gramps said.

Of course, Johnny and Louella received Christmas presents that Christmas too; but what they always remembered best was the gift of giving from their hearts – a gift for Gramps.

Aileen Fisher

Song suggestion

What shall I give to the child in the manger
(Carol gaily carol 26)

A New Doll

There was no trouble to get me off to bed that night. My Gramp said that he would be sure to see that the fire was out before he came to bed so that Father Christmas wouldn't burn himself when he came down the chimney. Hopefully I hung one of Gran's black stockings on the brass bed knob. Yet I wondered how Father Christmas would know that I was not still at Ducklington.

Next morning, almost before it was light, I crawled to the bottom of the bed. He had been. I could feel the knobbly, filled stocking. It was packed with things – sugar-mice, a liquorice pipe, nuts, an orange and a rosy apple, a painting book, a chocolate watch, like my Gramp wore in his

wesket pocket, and best of all, a beautiful little doll dressed in pink.

I squealed with delight – I had never had a real doll before, only black ones our Mother used to make from old stockings. My Gran found one of her crocheted shawls and I sat by the roaring fire nursing my lovely doll while she got on with the cooking.

Into the oven went the pheasant and potatoes for baking while on the hob a monstrous Christmas pudding bubbled and boiled in the great saucepan. Up to her elbows in flour, my Gran made pastry for mince pies. Her face was red and shiny where she kept bending and peering into the oven as each batch was drawn out.

For the hundredth time I peeped at my doll, then I let out a loud scream. 'What ever is the matter my little maid?' my Gran said, rushing over to my side.

'Look Granny, look,' I cried, my cheeks streaming with tears, 'my doll's face, it's gone.'

The heat from the fire had melted the pretty wax face; now all that was left was a shapeless lump. I cried for the rest of the day. I couldn't even eat. I never did taste the pheasant we had prepared so excitedly the day before. As my Gramp ate his Christmas pudding he kept finding shiny threepenny bits. 'Come on my little maid,' he said, 'you might find a florin in your piece.' But it was no use – nothing comforted me.

The next day one of the footmen from the big house knocked at the door of the lodge. He handed a big brown paper parcel to my Gran. 'It's for the little girl,' he said. We stood there for a moment, speechless. 'What ever is it Mr. Carter?' my Gran asked.

'Well Mrs. Broad, her ladyship heard that your little grandchild had had a most unfortunate accident with her doll. There's a note inside,' he said, and was gone.

Still bewildered we went back into the house and I snatched at the wrappings, tearing the paper with excited fingers. 'Careful, child,' my Gran warned, 'it might be something breakable.' She read the note pinned on the top of the box, 'For the pretty little girl in the gay green tammy'. Inside was the biggest, most beautiful doll I had ever seen. My Gran said that it must have belonged to one of her ladyship's children when they were small. It was dressed in fur-trimmed satin and all the clothes took off and I undressed that doll a hundred times or more that day I'm sure. Excitedly I told my Gramp about the doll when he came home from work. He lifted me on his lap and said, 'It's worth all the tea in China to see you laughing again.'

from A Kind of Magic *by Mollie Harris*

Papa Panov's Special Christmas

It was Christmas Eve and although it was still afternoon, lights had begun to appear in the shops and houses of the little Russian village, for the short winter day was nearly over. Excited children scurried indoors and now only muffled sounds of chatter and laughter escaped from closed shutters.

Old Papa Panov, the village shoemaker, stepped outside his shop to take one last look around. The sounds of happiness, the bright lights and the faint but delicious smells of Christmas cooking reminded him of past Christmas times when his wife had been alive and his own children little. Now they had gone. His usually cheerful face, with the little laughter wrinkles behind the round steel spectacles, looked sad now. But he went back indoors with a firm step, put up the shutters and set a pot of coffee to heat on the charcoal stove. Then, with a sigh, he settled in his big armchair.

Papa Panov did not often read, but tonight he pulled down the big old family Bible and, slowly tracing the lines with one forefinger, he read again the Christmas story. He read how Mary and Joseph, tired by their journey to Bethlehem, found no room for them at the inn, so that Mary's little baby was born in the cowshed.

'Oh dear, oh dear!' exclaimed Papa Panov, 'if only they had come here! I would have given them my bed and I could have covered the baby with my patchwork quilt to keep him warm.'

He read on about the wise men who had come to see the baby Jesus, bringing him splendid gifts. Papa Panov's face fell.

'I have no gift that I could give him,' he thought sadly.

Then his face brightened. He put down the Bible, got up and stretched his long arms to the shelf high up in his little room. He took down a small, dusty box and opened it. Inside was a perfect pair of tiny leather shoes. Papa Panov smil-ed with satisfaction. Yes, they were as good as he had remembered – the best shoes he had ever made.

'I should give him those,' he decided, as he gently put them away and sat down again.

He was feeling tired now, and the further he read the sleepier he became. The print began to dance before his eyes so that he closed them, just for a moment. In no time at all Papa Panov was fast asleep.

And as he slept he dreamed. He dreamed that someone was in his room and he knew at once, as one does in dreams, who the person was. It was Jesus.

'You have been wishing that you could see me, Papa Panov,' he said kindly, 'then look for me tomorrow. It will be Christmas Day and I will visit you. But look carefully, for I shall not tell you who I am.'

When at last Papa Panov awoke, the bells were ringing out and a thin light was filtering through the shutters.

'Bless my soul!' said Papa Panov. 'It's Christmas Day!'

He stood up and stretched himself for he was rather stiff. Then his face filled with happiness as he remembered his dream. This would be a very special Christmas after all, for Jesus was coming to visit him. How would he look? Would he be a little baby, as at that first Christmas? Would he be a grown man, a carpenter – or the great King that he is, God's Son? He must watch carefully the whole day through so that he recognised him however he came.

Papa Panov put on a special pot of coffee for his Christmas breakfast, took down the shutters and looked out of the window. The street was deserted,

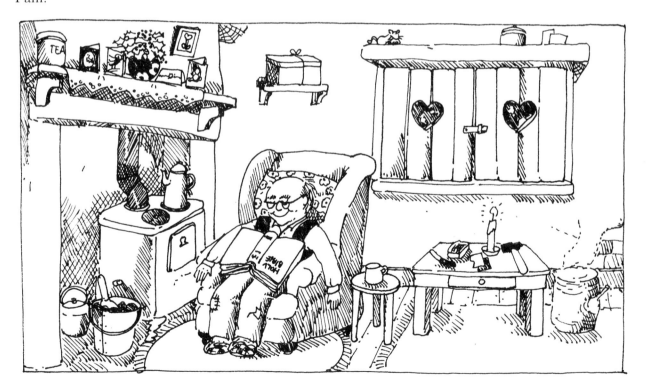

no one was stirring yet. No one except the road sweeper. He looked as miserable and dirty as ever, and well he might! Whoever wanted to work on Christmas Day – and in the raw cold and bitter freezing mist of such a morning?

Papa Panov opened the shop door, letting in a thin stream of cold air. 'Come in!' he shouted across the street cheerily. 'Come and have some hot coffee to keep out the cold!'

The sweeper looked up, scarcely able to believe his ears. He was only too glad to put down his broom and come into the warm room. His old clothes steamed gently in the heat of the stove and he clasped both red hands round the comforting warm mug as he drank.

Papa Panov watched him with satisfaction, but every now and then his eyes strayed to the window. It would never do to miss his special visitor.

'Expecting someone?' the sweeper asked at last. So Papa Panov told him about his dream. 'Well, I hope he comes,' the sweeper said, 'you've given me a bit of Christmas cheer I never expected to have. I'd say you deserve to have your dream come true.' And he actually smiled.

When he had gone, Papa Panov put on cabbage soup for his dinner, then went to the door again, scanning the street. He saw no one. But he was mistaken. Someone *was* coming.

The girl walked so slowly and quietly, hugging the walls of shops and houses, that it was a while before he noticed her. She looked very tired and she was carrying something. As she drew nearer he could see that it was a baby, wrapped in a thin shawl. There was such sadness in her face and in the pinched little face of the baby, that Papa Panov's heart went out to them.

'Won't you come in?' he called, stepping outside to meet them. 'You both need a warm by the fire and a rest.'

The young mother let him shepherd her indoors and to the comfort of the armchair. She gave a big sigh of relief.

'I'll warm some milk for the baby,' Papa Panov said, 'I've had children of my own – I can feed her for you.' He took the milk from the stove and carefully fed the baby from a spoon, warming her tiny feet by the stove at the same time.

'She needs shoes,' the cobbler said.

But the girl replied, 'I can't afford shoes, I've got no husband to bring home money. I'm on my way to the next village to get work.'

A sudden thought flashed into Papa Panov's mind. He remembered the little shoes he had looked at last night. But he had been keeping those for Jesus. He looked again at the cold little feet and made up his mind.

'Try these on her,' he said, handing the baby and the shoes to the mother. The beautiful little shoes were a perfect fit. The girl smiled happily and the baby gurgled with pleasure.

'You have been so kind to us,' the girl said, when she got up with her baby to go. 'May all your Christmas wishes come true!'

But Papa Panov was beginning to wonder if his very special Christmas wish *would* come true. Perhaps he had missed his visitor? He looked anxiously up and down the street. There were plenty of people about but they were all faces that he recognised. There were neighbours going to call on their families. They nodded and smiled and wished him Happy Christmas! Or beggars – and Papa Panov hurried indoors to fetch them hot soup and a generous hunk of bread, hurrying out again in case he missed the Important Stranger.

All too soon the winter dusk fell. When Papa Panov next went to the door and strained his eyes he could no longer make out the passers-by. Most were home and indoors by now anyway. He walked slowly back into his room at last, put up the shutters and sat down wearily in his armchair.

So it had been just a dream after all.

Jesus had not come.

Then all at once he knew that he was no longer alone in the room.

This was no dream for he was wide awake. At first he seemed to see before his eyes the long stream of people who had come to him that day. He saw again the old road sweeper, the young mother and her baby and the beggars he had fed. As they passed each whispered, 'Didn't you see *me*, Papa Panov?'

'Who are you?' he called out, bewildered.

Then another voice answered him. It was the voice from his dream – the voice of Jesus.

'I was hungry and you fed me,' he said. 'I was naked and you clothed me. I was cold and you warmed me. I came to you today in every one of those you helped and welcomed.'

Then all was quiet and still. Only the sound of the big clock ticking. A great peace and happiness seemed to fill the room, overflowing Papa Panov's heart until he wanted to burst out singing and laughing and dancing with joy.

'So he *did* come after all!' was all that he said.

Leo Tolstoy

Christmas Thank You's

Dear Auntie
Oh, what a nice jumper
I've always adored powder blue
and fancy you thinking of
orange and pink
for the stripes
how clever of you!

Dear Uncle
The soap is
terrific
So
useful
and such a kind thought and
how did you guess that
I'd just used the last of
the soap that last Christmas brought

Dear Gran
Many thanks for the hankies
Now I really can't wait for the flu
and the daisies embroidered
in red round the 'M'
for Michael
how
thoughtful of you!

Dear Cousin
What socks!
and the same sort you wear
so you must be
the last word in style
and I'm certain you're right that the
luminous green
will make me stand out a mile

Dear Sister
I quite understand your concern
it's a risk sending jam in the post
But I think I've pulled out
all the big bits
of glass
so it won't taste too sharp
spread on toast

    Dear Grandad
    Don't fret
    I'm delighted
    So *don't* think your gift will
    offend
    I'm not at all hurt
    that you gave up this year
    and just sent me
    a fiver
    to spend.

Mick Gowar

Afterthought

For weeks before it comes I feel excited, yet
    when it
At last arrives, things all go wrong:
My thoughts don't seem to fit.

I've planned what I'll give everyone and what
    they'll give to me,
And then on Christmas morning all
The presents seem to be

Useless and tarnished. I have dreamt that
    everything would come
To life – presents and people too.
Instead of that, I'm dumb,

And people say, 'How horrid! What a sulky
    little boy!'
And they are right. I *can't* seem pleased.
The lovely shining toy

I wanted so much when I saw it in a
    magazine
Seems pointless now. And Christmas too
No longer seems to mean

The hush, the star, the baby, the people being
    kind again.
The bells are rung, sledges are drawn,
And peace on earth for men.

Elizabeth Jennings

Acknowledgements

The publishers would like particularly to thank Peggy Blakeley for her help in compiling this book.

The following have kindly granted their permission for the reprinting of copyright material:

Afterthought from *The Secret Brother* by Elizabeth Jennings (Macmillan): David Higham Associates Ltd

Anansi at Christmas (A story for Christmas) from *Hand in Hand Assembly Book* by R. Profitt: Longman Group Ltd

The Big White Pussy-cat from *Folk Tales* by Leila Berg: Hodder & Stoughton Children's Books

The Brave Robin by Noel Barr: Reproduced from the former Ladybird title *The Wise Robin* by Noel Barr with the permission of the publishers, Ladybird Books Ltd., Loughborough, England

A Busy Day from *More William* by Richmal Crompton: Macmillan, London and Basingstoke

Cardboard cylinder figures and **Paper bag figures** (Figures for a Nativity scene) from *Bright Ideas for Christmas Art and Craft* (p 40): Scholastic Publications Ltd

Charades and word games (Christmas charades) by Roberta Warman from *Junior Education*: Scholastic Publications Ltd

Charlie Wag and three riddles from *The Oxford Nursery Rhyme Book* assembled by Iona and Peter Opie (1955): Oxford University Press

Christmas costumes (Sew something simple) from *Hands Together* November 1984: Scholastic Publications Ltd

Christmas Eve from *The Magic Apple Tree* by Susan Hill: Hamish Hamilton Ltd

Christmas is in the air from *Roundabout* by Alison Winn: Hodder & Stoughton Children's Books

Christmas Thank You's from *Swings and Roundabouts* by Mick Gowar: Collins Publishers, © Mick Gowar 1981

Cider with Rosie (two extracts) by Laurie Lee: Chatto & Windus, The Hogarth Press

The Computer's First Christmas Card from *Poems of Thirty Years* by Edwin Morgan (1982): Carcanet Press Ltd, Manchester

Diary of a farmer's wife (two extracts) by Jean Preston (Allen Lane, 1980): Reproduced by permission of Penguin Books Ltd, © Mollie Preston 1937, 1964, 1980

End of term from *Farmer's Boy* by John R. Allan: Century Hutchinson Ltd

Father Christmas and the Carpenter by Alf Prøysen: Century Hutchinson Ltd

Father Christmas's Clothes by Paul Biegel, translated by Patricia Crampton: Glover & Blair Ltd, Bristol

First Snow from *A Pocketful of Poems* by Marie Louise Allen: © 1939 Harper & Row Publishers Inc. © 1957 Marie Allen Howarth. Reprinted by permission of Harper & Row Publishers Inc

A Gift for Gramps by Aileen Fisher: By permission of the author

Horace's Christmas Disappointment by Anthony Thwaite: By permission of the author

Hugo at Sky Castle from *Hugo and the Wicked Winter* by Tony Ross: By permission of the author

Ideas for Christmas Cards from *All the year round* by Toni Arthur (Puffin Books, 1981): Reproduced by permission of Penguin Books Ltd, © Toni Arthur 1981

If Santa Claus comes down the chimney by John P. Long and Fred Gibson: © 1935 Francis Day & Hunter Ltd. Used by permission of EMI Music Publishing Ltd, London WC2H 0LD

In the Wood by Eileen Mathias: Bell & Hyman Publishers

Jelly case angel from *Bright Ideas for Christmas Art and Craft*: Scholastic Publications Ltd

The Kings by Peter Cornelius, translated by H. N. Bate: Oxford University Press Music Dept

Legend of the Spider's Web from *The Daily Study Bible (Matthew, vol 1)* by William Barclay: The Church of Scotland, The Saint Andrew Press, Edinburgh

Loop mobiles (Ribbon loops) from *Bright Ideas for Christmas Art and Craft*: Scholastic Publications Ltd

Mincemeat slices from the recipe by Delia Smith, *Radio Times* 14th December 1985: by kind permission of Deborah Owen Ltd, © Delia Smith 1985

Morris's Disappearing Bag by Rosemary Wells (Kestrel Books, 1977): © Rosemary Wells, 1975. Reproduced by permission of Penguin Books Ltd, and by permission of the publisher, Dial Books for Young Readers

Mrs Malone from *Silver Sand and Snow* by Eleanor Farjeon (Michael Joseph): David Higham Associates Ltd

A New Doll from *A Kind of Magic* by Mollie Harris: Chatto & Windus

Paul's Christmas Birthday by Carol Garrick: William Morrow & Co Inc, New York

A Pop-up Card from *The Christmas Book* by Susan Baker: Macdonald Educational

Rama The drawing on page 22 is by Kay Ambrose, from *Classical dances and costumes of India* by Kay Ambrose and Ram Gopal, A & C Black, 1983.

The Redbreast from *The Inn of the Birds* by Anthony Rye: Reprinted by arrangement with Jonathan Cape Ltd

The Robots' Christmas Dinner by Jan Holdstock: Universal Edition (London) Ltd

The Royal Christmas Tree (picture on page 88): BBC Hulton Picture Library

Shops at Christmas by Janis Baker, from *From a Busy Hubbub* Poems by children, chosen by Margot Chahin and John Lloyd: Collins. Poems © William Collins Sons & Co Ltd 1969

Sir Oswald (Story Time) from *All the year round* by Toni Arthur (Puffin Books, 1981): Reproduced by permission of Penguin Books Ltd. © Toni Arthur 1981

Snow by Leonard Clark: By permission of the Literary Executor of the author

Snowfall from *Farther than far* by Margaret Hillert: Used by permission of the author who controls all rights

The Snow Queen's Palace from *The Snow Queen* by Hans Christian Andersen: Reproduced by permission of Hamlyn Publishing, a division of the Hamlyn Publishing Group Ltd

Snow Stars by Frances Frost from *Pictures and stories* by Arnold Arnold: Dover Publications Inc, New York

Snow Toward Evening from *So that it flower* by Melville Cane: © 1926 Harcourt Brace Jovanovich Inc, renewed 1954 by Melville Cane. By permission of Harcourt Brace Jovanovich Inc, Orlando, Florida

Star blaze by Douglas Coombes from *Lindsay Carol Book 1*: Lindsay Music, Biggleswade

Up on the moon by Nona Maiola from *A Child's Treasury of Verse*: Hodder & Stoughton Children's Books

We have come to Bethlehem from *Eight days to Christmas* by Geraldine Kaye: Macmillan, London and Basingstoke

The White Robin (extract) by Miss Read: Michael Joseph Ltd

Why a donkey was chosen by Christopher Gregorowski: Curtis Brown Group Ltd, © Christopher Gregorowski 1975, first published by Ernest Benn Ltd

Winter Days from *Salford Road* by Gareth Owen: By permission of the author

Winter Morning by Ogden Nash: © Ogden Nash. Reproduced by permission of Curtis Brown Ltd, London

Winter Morning by Clive Sansom: By permission of Ruth Samsom

Every effort has been made to trace and acknowledge copyright owners. If any right has been omitted, the publishers offer their apologies and will rectify this in subsequent editions following notification.

Index of authors

Alcott, Louisa M.
Angels in hoods and mittens,   97

Allan, John R.
End of term,   61

Allen, Marie Louise
First Snow,   14

Andersen, Hans Christian
The Snow Queen's Palace,   9

Arthur, Toni
Sir Oswald,   39

Baker, Janis
Shops at Christmas,   96

Barclay, William
The Legend of the Spider's
Web,   82

Barr, Noel
The Brave Robin,   70

Berg, Leila
The Big White Pussy-cat,   76

Biegel, Paul
Father Christmas's Clothes,   34

Bijlani, Judith
Diwali in Bombay,   22

Bluer, Andy
The Lighthouse Keeper's
Christmas,   19

Cane, Melville
Snow Toward Evening,   5

Chandrasiri, Chalene
The New Baby King,   92

Clark, Leonard
Snow,   5

Cornelius, Peter
The Kings,   40

Crompton, Richmal
A Busy Day,   96

Dickens, Charles
A Christmas Carol
(excerpts),   11, 41, 60

Farjeon, Eleanor
Mrs Malone,   80

Fisher, Aileen
A Gift for Gramps,   104

Frost, Frances
Snow stars,   10

Garrick, Carol
Paul's Christmas Birthday,   46

Gowar, Mick
Christmas Thank You's,   108

Grahame, Kenneth
Carols at Mole End,   49
Snow arrives in the Wild
Wood,   7

Gregorowski, Christopher
Why a donkey was chosen,   73

Grimm, the brothers
The Elves and the Shoemaker,   102

Harris, Mollie
A New Doll,   105

Herrick, Robert
Hesperides (excerpt),   49
Twelfe Night (excerpt),   66

Hill, Susan
Christmas Eve,   63

Hillert, Margaret
Snowfall,   5

Holdstock, Jan
The Robots' Christmas
Dinner,   57

Jennings, Elizabeth
Afterthought,   108

Kaye, Geraldine
We have come to Bethlehem,   43

Lear, Edward
There was an old person
of Mold,   14

Lee, B.J.
Christmas Tree,   85

Lee, Laurie
Cider with Rosie (excerpts),   11, 48

Lewis, Phyllis
The most memorable snowfall
of my life,   10

McKay, Mahes
Our hospital Christmas,   50

Maiola, Nona
Up on the moon,   32

Mathias, Eileen
In the wood,   8

Morgan, Edwin
The Computer's First Christmas
Card,   101

Nash, Ogden
Winter Morning,   5

Neale, John
Good King Wenceslas,   35

Owen, Gareth
Winter Days,   13

Parekh, Michelle
The New Baby King,   92

Poon, Edwin
Our Chinese New Year,   56

Prøysen, Alf
Father Christmas and the
Carpenter,   27

Read, Miss
The White Robin,   69

Rosen, Mark
Does Christmas mean winter?   11

Ross, Tony
Hugo at Sky Castle,   78

Rossetti, Christina
Give me holly, bold and jolly,   91

Rye, Anthony
The Redbreast,   69

St. Joseph, David
Farming at Christmas,   82

Sansom, Clive
Winter Morning,   14

Snape, Marie
Christmas at school,   43

Thwaite, Anthony
Horace's Christmas
Disappointment,   103

Tolstoy, Leo
Papa Panov's Special
Christmas,   106

Weintroub, Barbara
Hanukkah,   23

Wells, Rosemary
Morris's Disappearing Bag,   93

Winn, Alison
Christmas is in the air,   85

Alphabetical list of contents

Activities

Acrostics, 16
Advent calendar, 42
Bird mobile, 72
Cardboard cylinder figures, 40
Cardboard roll tree, 83
Charades and word games, 51
Christmas costumes, 36
Christmas tree card, 89
Circular angel, 38
Circular robin, 67
Clay Christmas tree cards, 84
Egg box lanterns, 18
Heart baskets, 101
Ideas for Christmas cards, 98
Jelly case angel, 39
Knitted Father Christmas, 33
Knitted Teddy, 95
Lanterns, 26
Letter to Father Christmas, 32
Loop mobiles, 52
Making a forest picture or frieze, 8
Mistletoe kissing bough, 90
Model animals for the stable scene, 73
My New Year resolutions, 56
Paper bag figures, 40
Paper plate calendars, 98
Paper tree, 85
Pentagon star, 15
Pop-up card, A, 99
Remembering the birds, 71
Rocking Reindeer, 74
Sewn Christmas card, 100
Silver snowflakes for the Christmas tree, 87
Star-shaped Santa, 32
Tree mobile, 85

Information

Apple-howling, 49
Bean cake, 66
Boxing Day, 52
Carols and carol singing, 48
Christmas across Europe, 52
Christmas cards, 98
Christmas puddings, 62
Christmas tree, The, 88
Christmas tree and its relations, the, 91
Christmas tree lights, 25
Crackers, 50

Diwali, 22
Dumb cakes, 66
Epiphany and Twelfth Night, 53
Fire flowers, 25
Frumenty, 63
Good King Wenceslas, 35
Holly, ivy – evergreens, 91
Lord of Misrule, The, 53
Meat, 63
Mince Pies, 63
Mistletoe, 90
Mummers, 53
New Year's Eve, 56
Pantomimes, 53
Regent Street lights, 16
Reindeer, 75
Robin, The, 68
Saturnalia, 52
Snapdragon, 66
Stir-up Sunday, 66
Yule log, The, 91

Personal accounts

Christmas at school, 43
Diwali in Bombay, 22
Does Christmas mean Winter?, 11
Farming at Christmas, 82
Hanukkah, 23
Lighthouse Keeper's Christmas, The, 19
Most memorable snowfall of my life, The, 10
Our Chinese New Year, 56
Our hospital Christmas, 50

Poems

Afterthought (Jennings), 108
Charlie Wag, 62
Christmas is in the air (Winn), 85
Christmas Thank You's (Gowar), 108
Christmas Tree (Lee), 85
Computer's first Christmas Card, The (Morgan), 101
First Snow (Allen), 14
Flour of England, fruit of Spain, 62
Gathering round the Crib, The, 53
Give me holly, bold and jolly (Rossetti), 91
Good King Wenceslas (Neale), 35
Here he comes with his flaming bowl, 66

Highty tighty, paradighty, 91
Horace's Christmas Disappointment (Thwaite), 103
I'm called by the name of a man, 69
In the Wood (Mathias), 8
Kings, The (Cornelius), 40
Mrs Malone (Farjeon), 80
Night in Bethlehem, 10
Now, now the mirth comes (Herrick), 66
Redbreast, The (Rye), 69
Robin's Song, 68
Robots' Christmas Dinner, The (Holdstock), 57
Shops at Christmas (Baker), 96
Snow (Clark), 5
Snowfall (Hillert), 5
Snow stars (Frost), 10
Snow Toward Evening (Cane), 5
Spring has now unwrapped the flowers, 35
Stand fast, root, bear well, top, 49
Star light, star bright, 23
There was an old person of Mold (Lear), 14
Up on the moon (Maiola), 32
Wassail the trees that they may beare (Herrick), 49
We wish you a merry Christmas, 62
Winter Days (Owen), 13
Winter Morning (Nash), 5
Winter Morning (Sansom), 14
Winter's Day, A, 8

Recipes

Chocolate and coconut shortbread, 95
Chocolate truffles, 103
Christmas tree biscuits, 84
Mincemeat slices, 65
Peppermint fondant creams, 103
St. Nicholas letter biscuits, 62
Surprise Christmas Pud, 57

Songs

Christmas echo song, 54
Christmas Eve, 44
Christmas food song, 58
Christmas tree, straight and tall, 86
Five jolly snowmen, 14
If Santa Claus comes down the chimney, 30

Let's make a party hat, 47
Mince pie calypso, 64
Pass the parcel, 94
Robin Redbreast, 68
Shepherds wake, 37
Snow, 12
Snow echo song, 6
Star blaze, 24
Star in the velvet sky, 18

Stories and extracts

Anansi at Christmas, 76
Angels in hoods and mittens (Alcott), 97
Baboushka, 41
Big White Pussy-cat, The (Berg), 76
Brave Robin, The (Barr), 70
Busy Day, A (Crompton), 96
Carols at Mole End (Grahame), 49
Christmas Dinner, The (Dickens), 60
Christmas Eve (Hill), 63
Diary of a farmer's wife, 60
Elves and the Shoemaker, The (Grimm), 102
End of term (Allan), 61
Father Christmas and the Carpenter (Prøysen), 27
Father Christmas's Clothes (Biegel), 34
First call: the Squire's house (Lee), 48
Game of Popp, The, 50
Gift for Gramps, A (Fisher), 104
Hugo at Sky Castle (Ross), 78
Legend of the Spider's Web (Barclay), 82
Morris's Disappearing Bag (Wells), 93
New Baby King, The, 92
New Doll, A (Harris), 105
Papa Panov's Special Christmas (Tolstoy), 106
Paul's Christmas Birthday (Garrick), 46
Scrooge and his nephew (Dickens), 41
Sir Oswald (Arthur), 39
Snow arrives in the Wild Wood (Grahame), 7
Snow Queen's Palace, The (Andersen), 9
We have come to Bethlehem (Kaye), 43
White Robin, The (Read), 69
Why a donkey was chosen (Gregorowski), 73
Winter in town and country (Lee; Grahame), 11

Subject Index

See page 110 for an index of authors, and page 111 for an alphabetical list of contents, grouped into Activities, Poems, Stories etc.

Acrostics 16
Advent Calendar 42, 43
All-Hallows Eve 53
Anansi 76
Angels
  activities 36, 38, 39
  stories 92, 97
Apple-howling 49
Baboushka 41
Bean Cake 53, 66
Befana 52
Bell-ringing 56
Bethlehem 10, 18, 37, 40, 41, 43
Boxing Day 52
Calendars
  activities 42, 98
Canada 75
Candles 17, 23, 25, 52
Carols, carol-singing
  info 35, 48, 88
  stories 21, 48, 49, 63
Charades 51
China 56
Christmas cake
  activity 57
  song 58
  story 60
Christmas cards
  activities 84, 89, 98, 99, 100
  info 98
  poem 101
Christmas dinner 21
  info 63
  poem 57

song 58
stories 60, 76
Christmas Eve
  info 66
  song 44
  story 63
Christmas pudding
  activity 57, 98
  info 62
  poem 62
  songs 58, 62
  story 60
Christmas tree
  activities 83, 84, 85, 89, 100
  info 88, 91
  poems 85
  song 86
  story 70
Clothes
  activities 36, 40
  poems 14, 96, 108
  song 47
  stories 34, 102
Conifers 91
Crackers 20, 21, 50
Cromwell, Oliver 53, 63
Decorations 20
  activities 15, 18, 26, 32, 38, 39, 42, 52, 67, 72, 74, 83, 84, 85, 87, 90
  info 16, 25
  song 86
  story 70
Diwali 22
Donkey 52, 92
  story 73
Dumb Cakes 66
Epiphany 52, 53, 66
Eskimos 75
Father Christmas
  activities 32, 33, 98
  info 52, 75
  poem 32

song 30
stories 27, 34, 46
Fire-flowers 25
First-footing 56
Fish 56, 63
France 52
Frost
  poem 13
  song 12
  story 11
Frumenty 63
Games 23
  activities 51
  song 94
  story 50
Germany 52, 88
Guyana 76
Hanukkah 22, 23
Herod 82
Hogmanay 56
Holland 52, 62
Holly 91, 98
Hospital 50
Ice
  song 12
  stories 9, 11, 78
India 22
Italy 52
Ivy 91
Kings
  activity 57
  info 52, 53, 66
  poem 40
  song 18
  stories 41, 43, 92
Lakshmi 22
Lanterns
  activities 18, 26
Lapps 75
Lighthouse-keeper
  story 19

Lord of Misrule 53, 66
Magi – see Kings
Meat 62, 63
Meat cake 50, 60
Mexico 25
Mince pies
  info 63
  songs 58, 64
  stories 60, 63
Mistletoe
  activity 90
  info 56, 90
Mummers 53
New Year resolutions 56
New Year's Day 11, 22, 56
New Year's Eve 56
Northern Lights, the 9
Norway 88
Norway Spruce 91
Pantomimes
  info 53
  story 76
Papua New Guinea 11
Parties
  song 47
  stories 46, 50
Poinsettias 25
Poland 52
Popp 50
Queen's Speech 21
Rama 22
Regent Street lights 16
Reindeer
  activity 74
  info 75
Robins
  activity 67
  info 68
  poems 68, 69
  song 68
  stories 69, 70
St. Lucia 52